# makrōfəˈtägrəfē
## macro photography

A larger than life album of small living things.

## makrōfəˈtägrəfē | macro photography

a larger than life album of small living things

Copyright © 2018 by Therese Holthausen. All rights reserved.

No part of this book may be reproduced or transmitted in any form or by any means, electronic or mechanical, including photocopying, recording or by any manner whatsoever without the express written permission of the publisher

First Printing, 2018
ISBN: 9781728965666

Printed in the United States of America.

T. Holthausen
PO Box 8375, Portland, OR 97207
holthausenpublishing@gmail.com

## Sincere Thank You to...

Mother Nature
for providing beauty and inspiration

Guus (daddy), for always being proud of me

J.C. and our fur kids
Kona, Max, Prefontaine, Dalai, Sym & Mira
my source of pure joy and unconditional love

YOU
for supporting my passion and this labor of love.

makrōfə'tägrəfē                                                                                                                                                          macrophotography

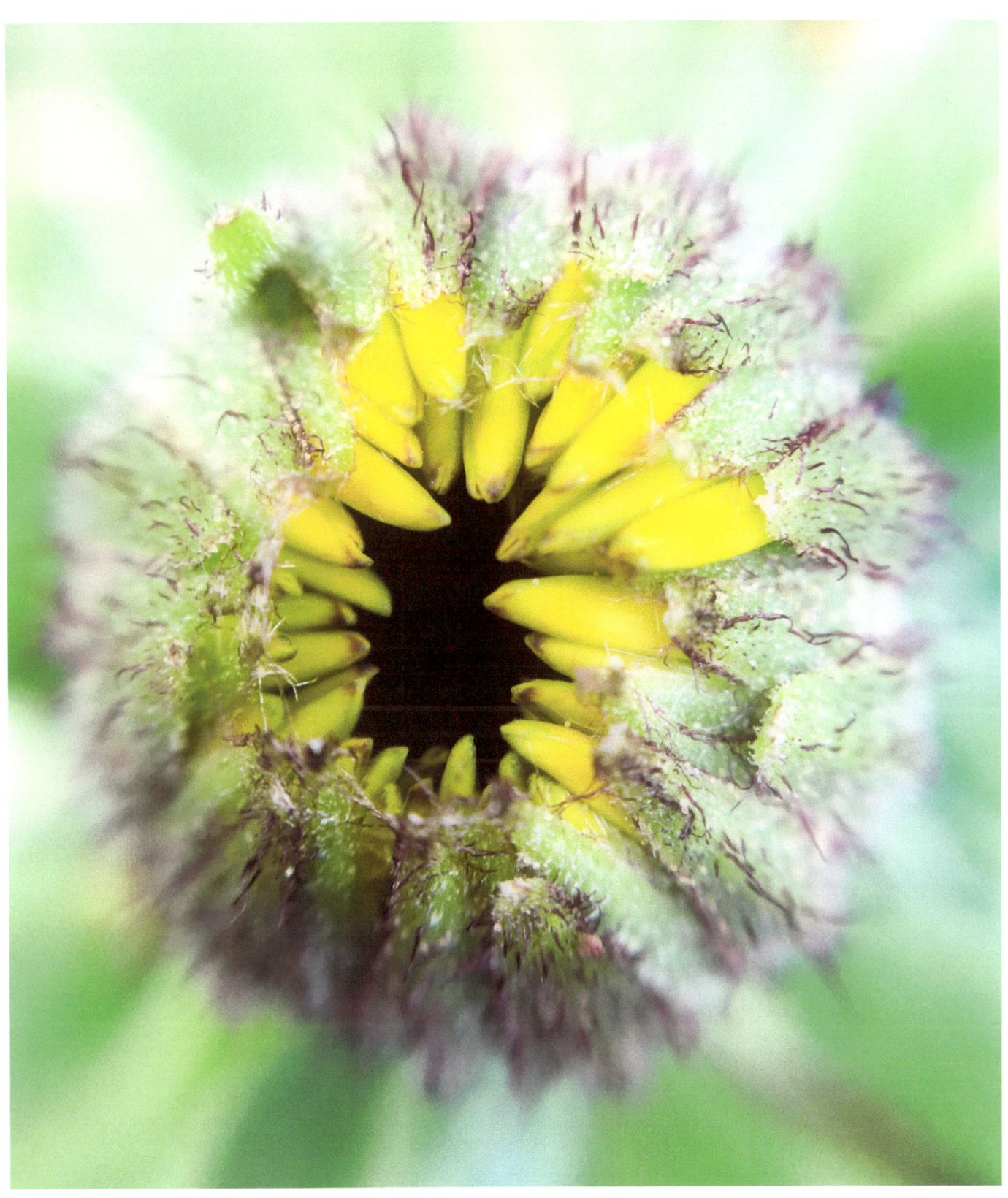

makrōfəˈtägrəfē / macrophotography

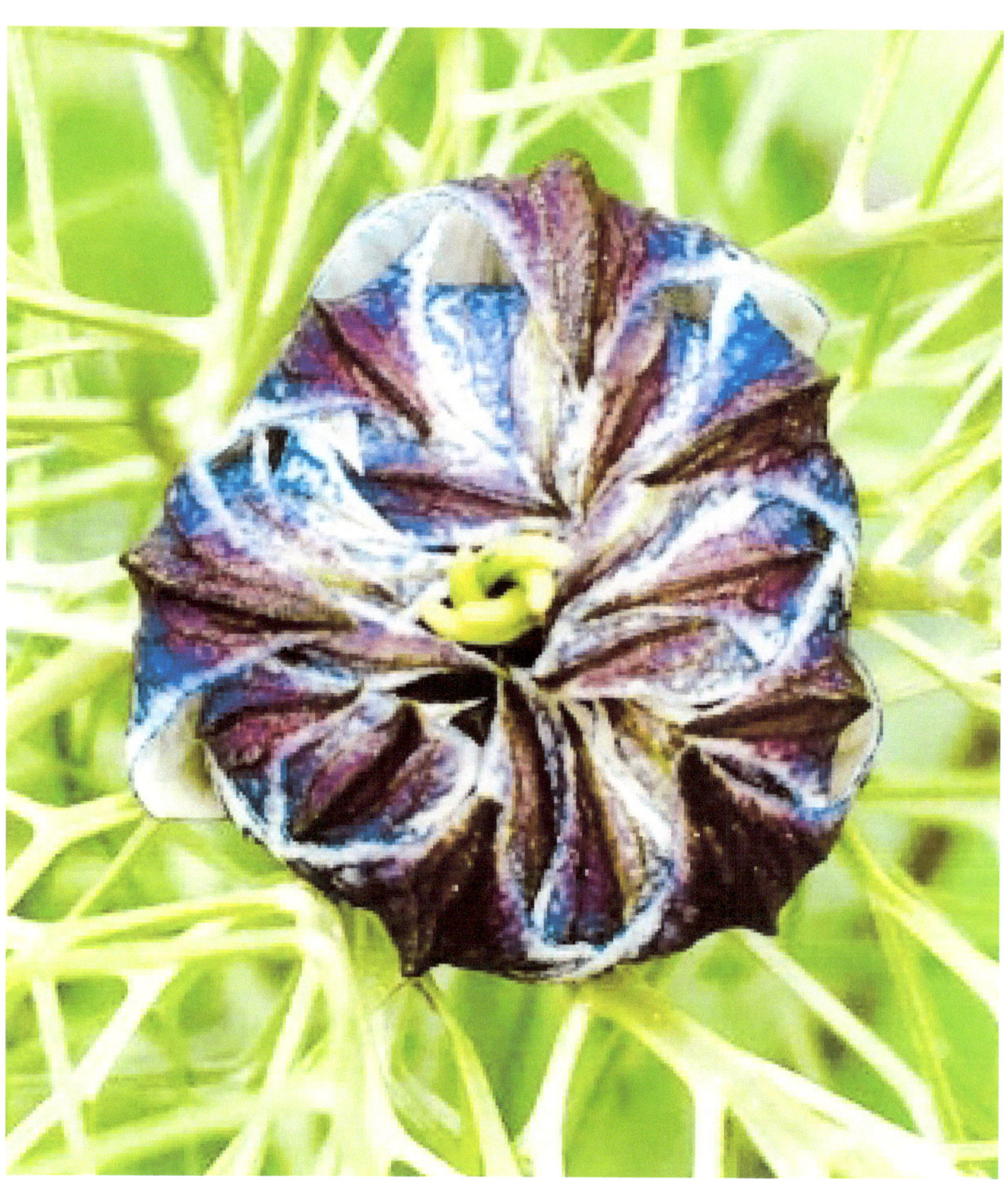

makrōfəˈtägrəfē     macrophotography

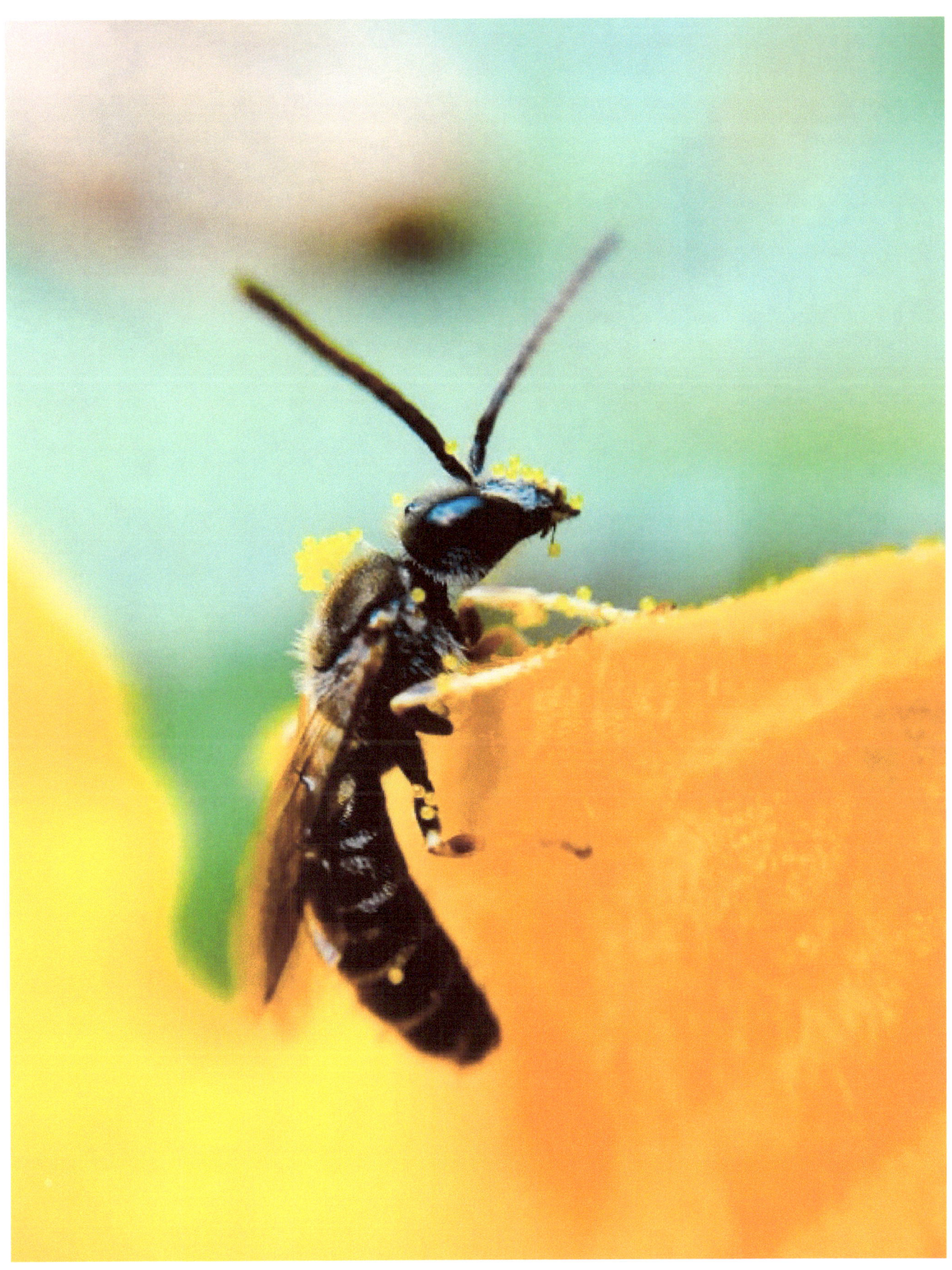

makrōfəˈtägrəfē macrophotography

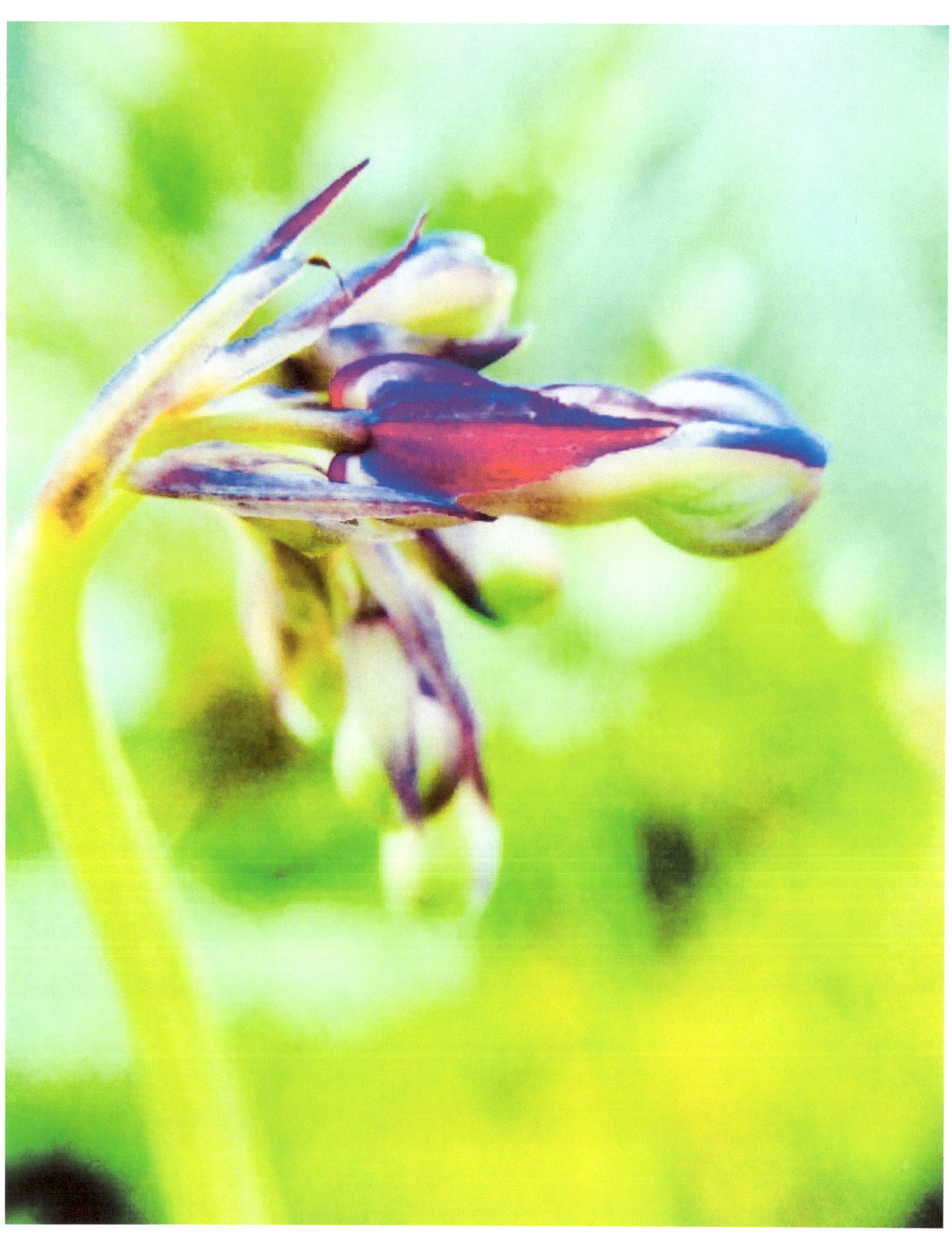

makrōfəˈtägrəfē macrophotography

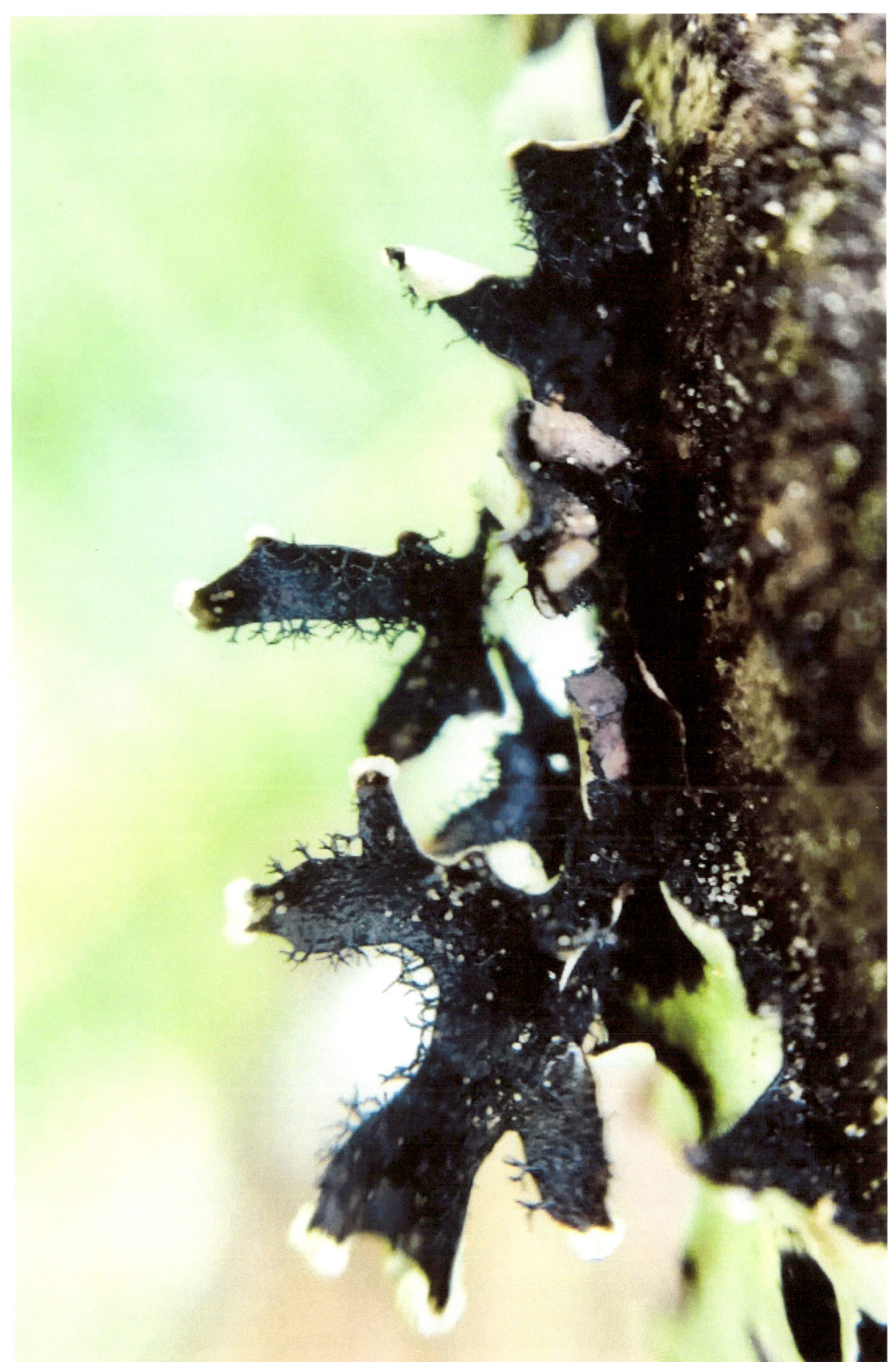

makrōfəˈtägrəfē                                                                                       macrophotography

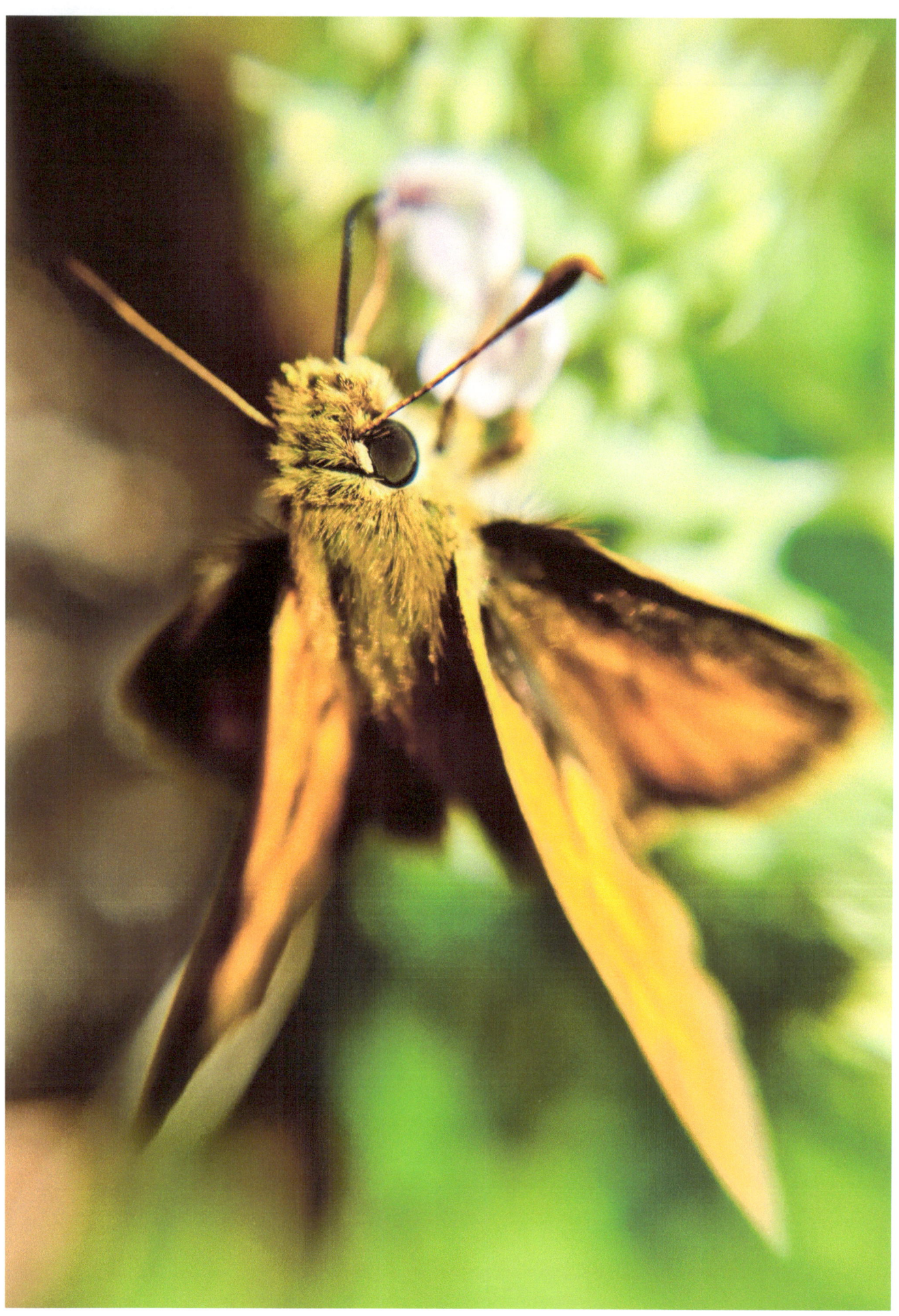

makrōfəˈtägrəfē  macrophotography

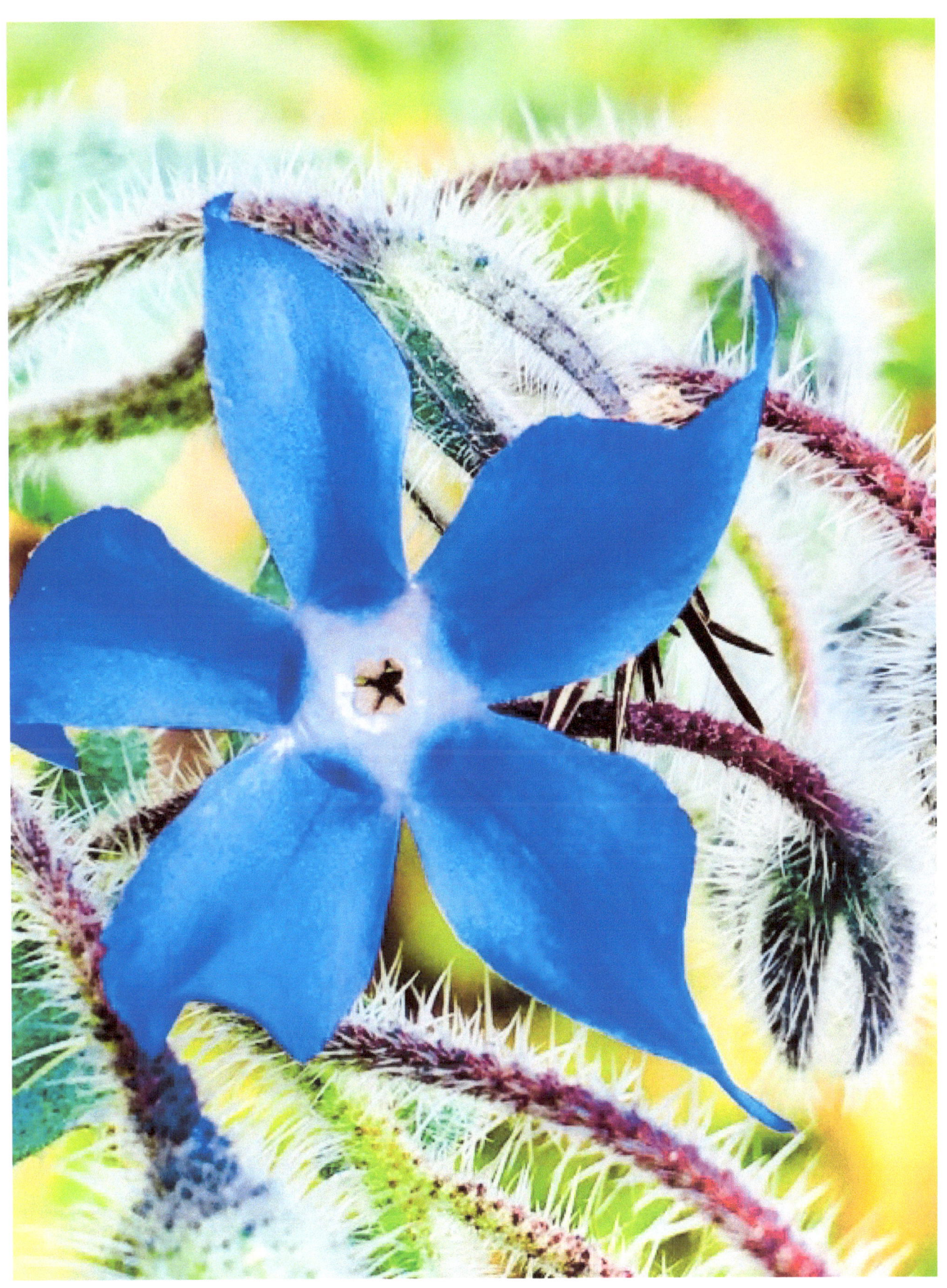

makrōfəˈtägrəfē     macrophotography

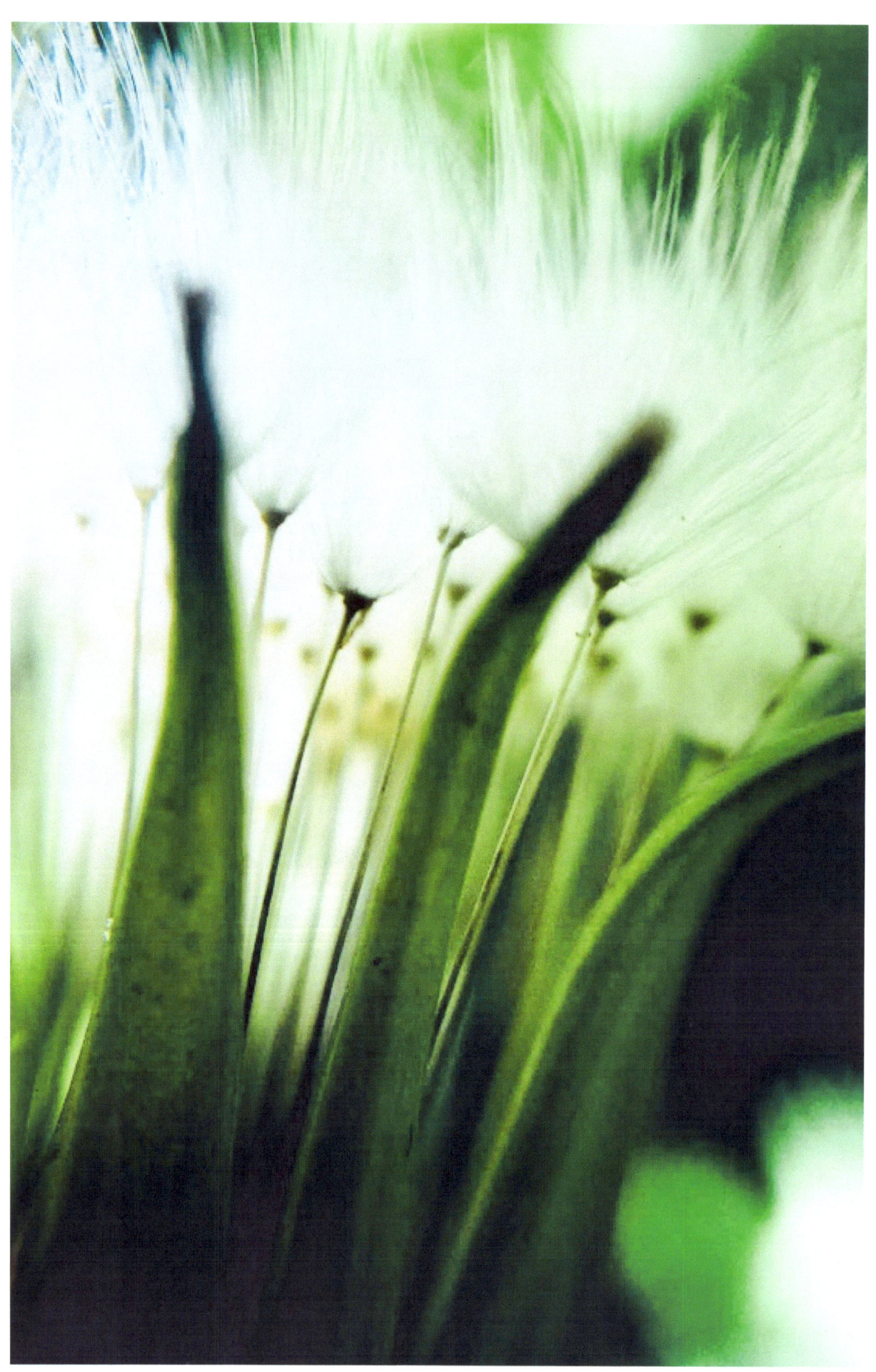

makrōfəˈtägrəfē macrophotography

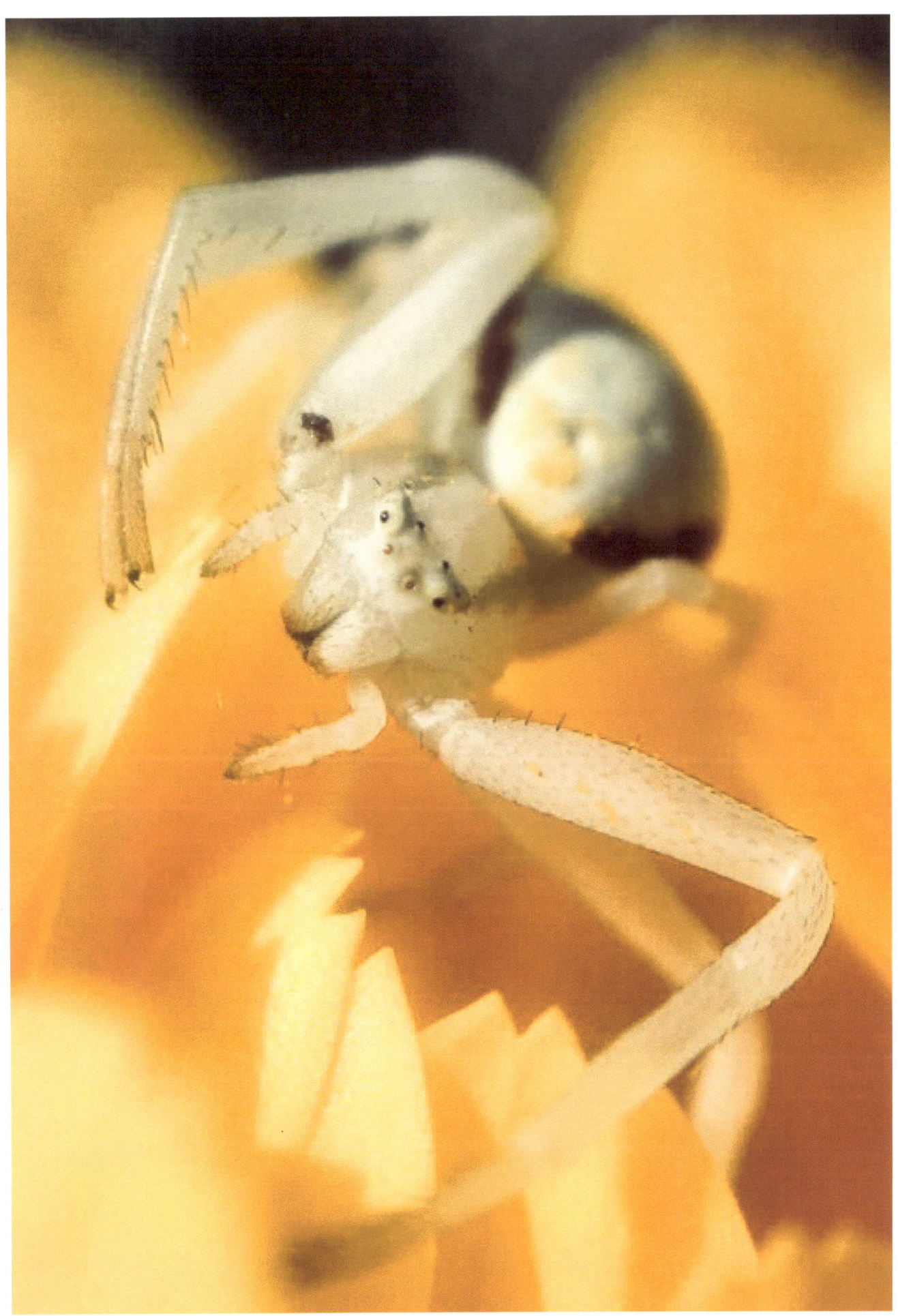

makrōfəˈtägrəfē · macrophotography

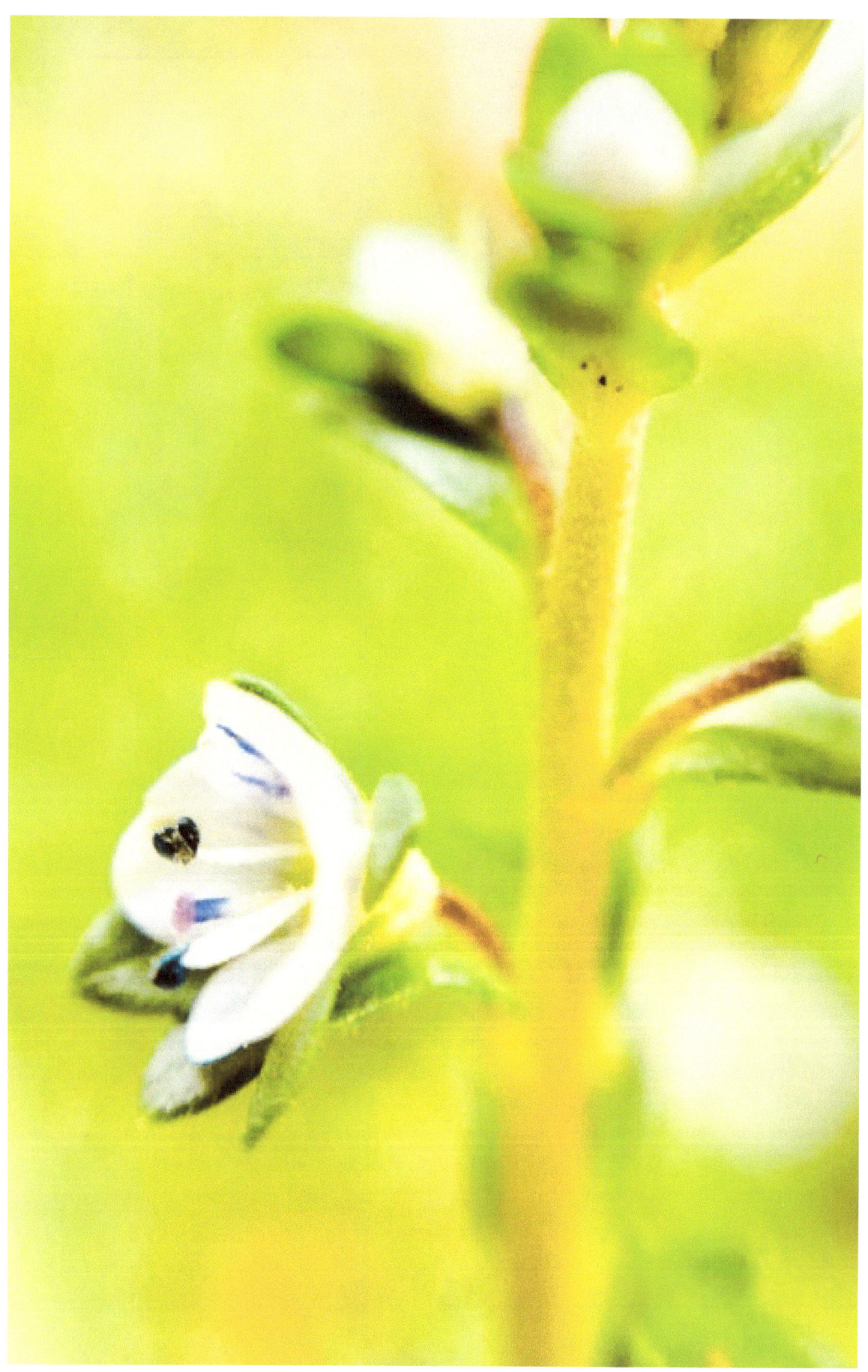

makrōfəˈtägrəfē    macrophotography

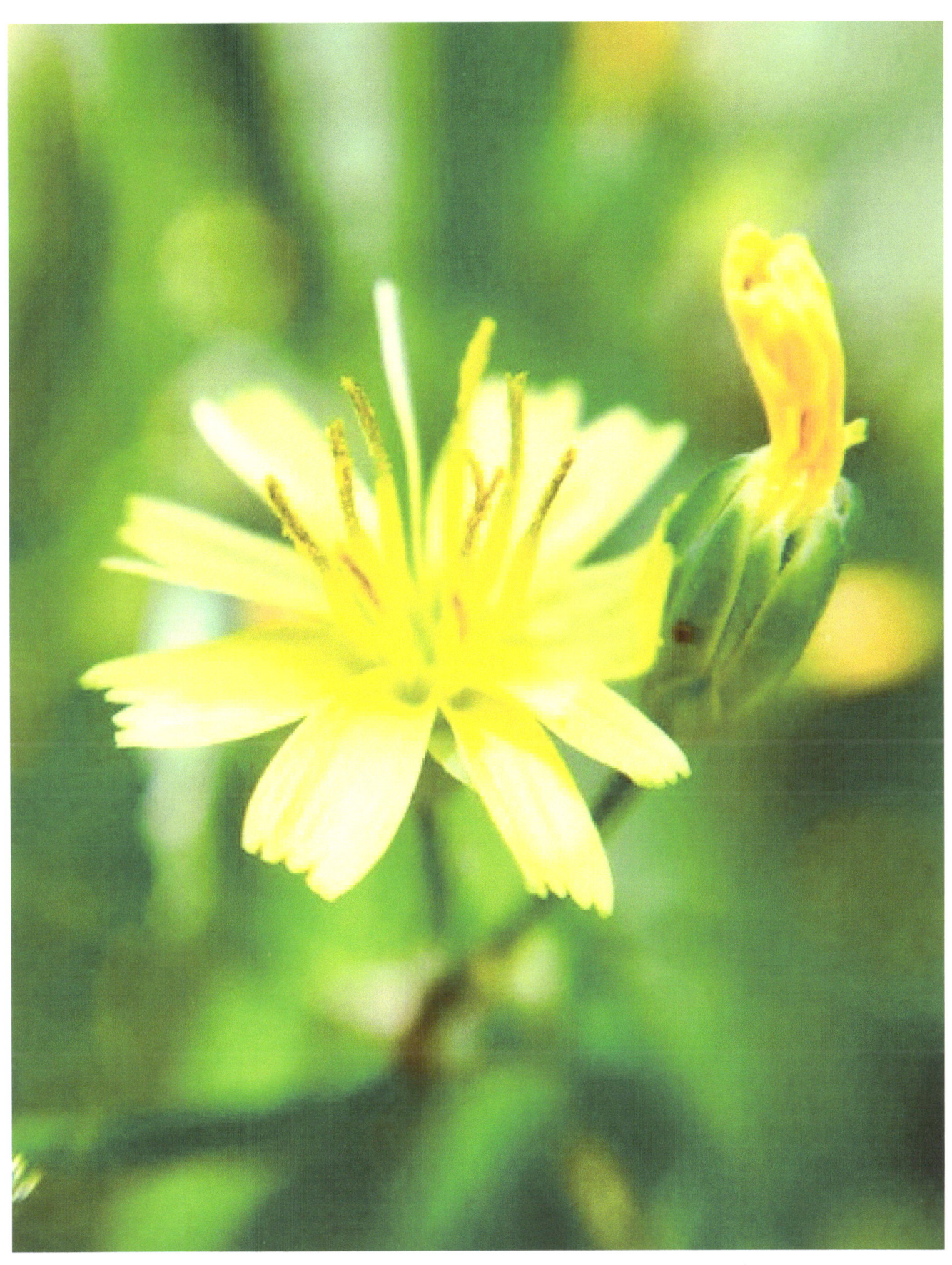

makrōfəˈtägrəfē · macrophotography

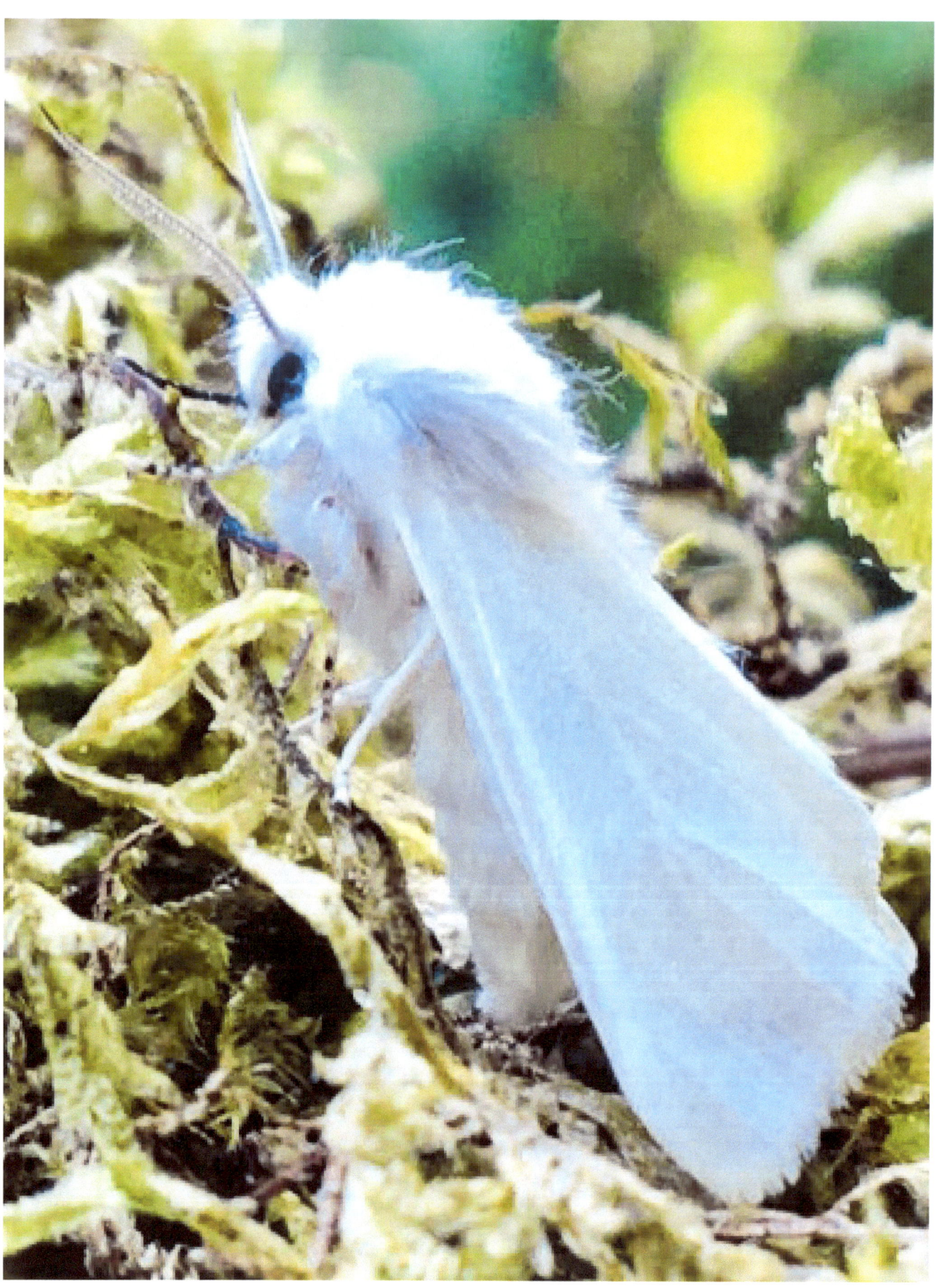

makrōfəˈtägrəfē                              macrophotography

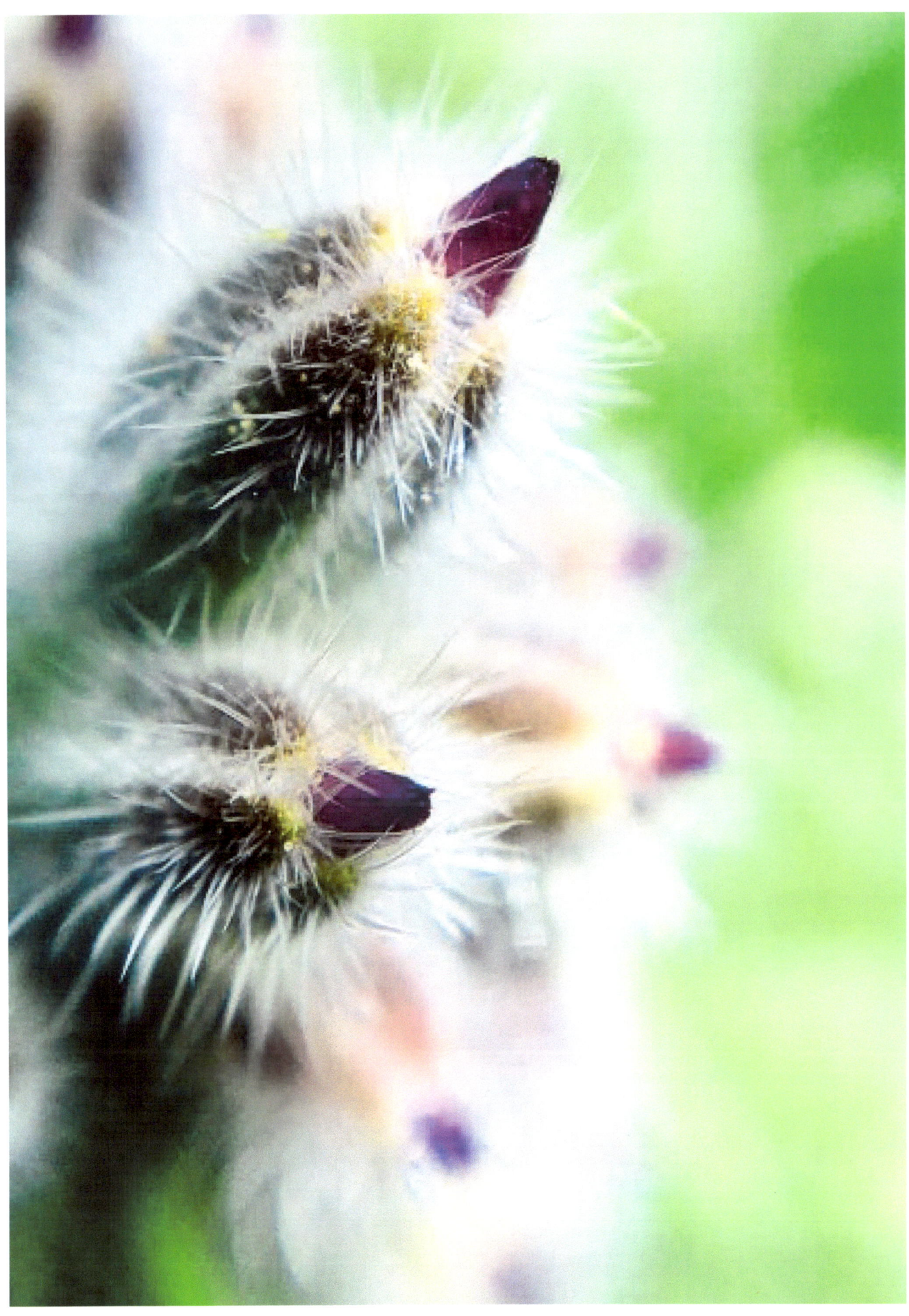

makrōfəˈtägrəfē · macrophotography

makrōfəˈtägrəfē

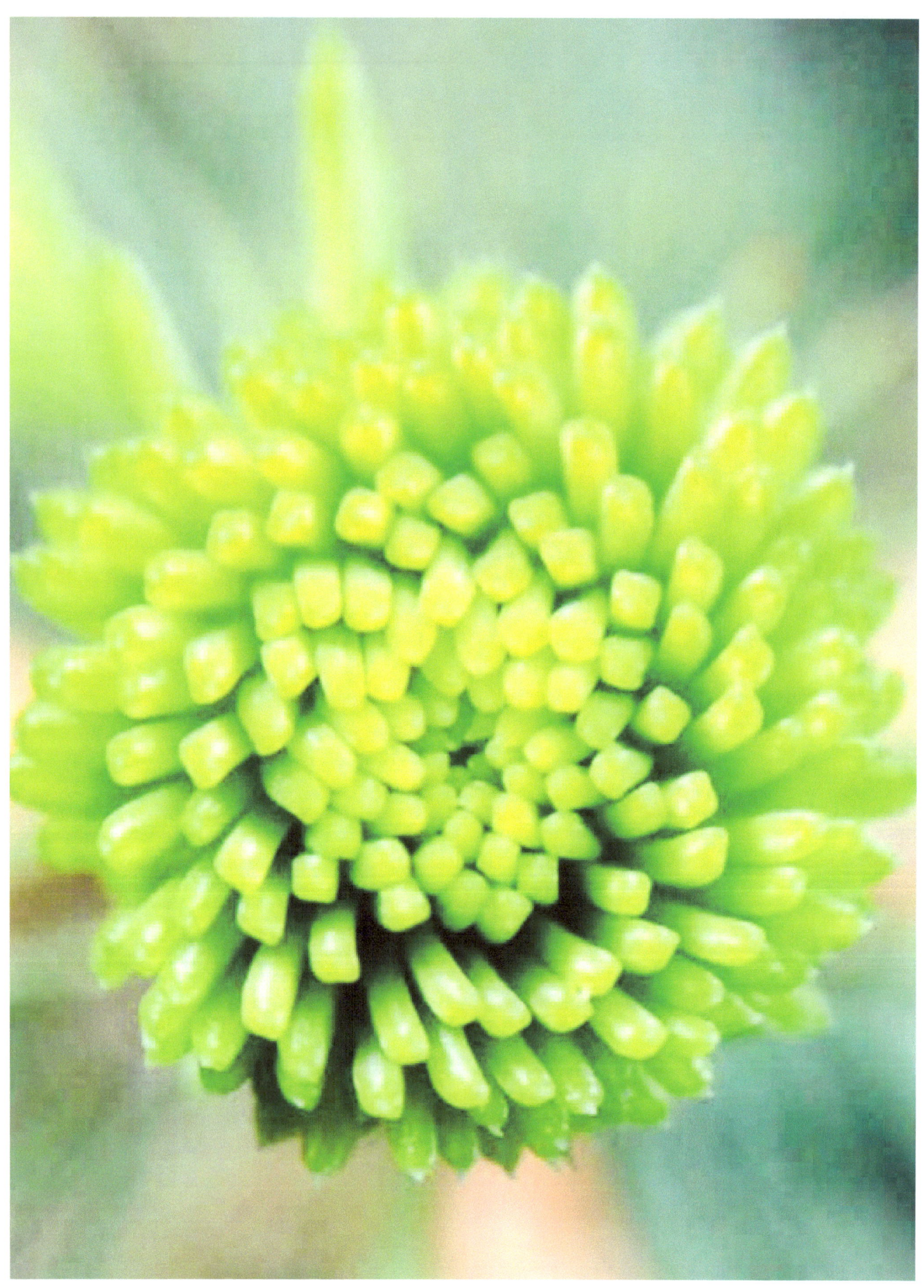

macrophotography

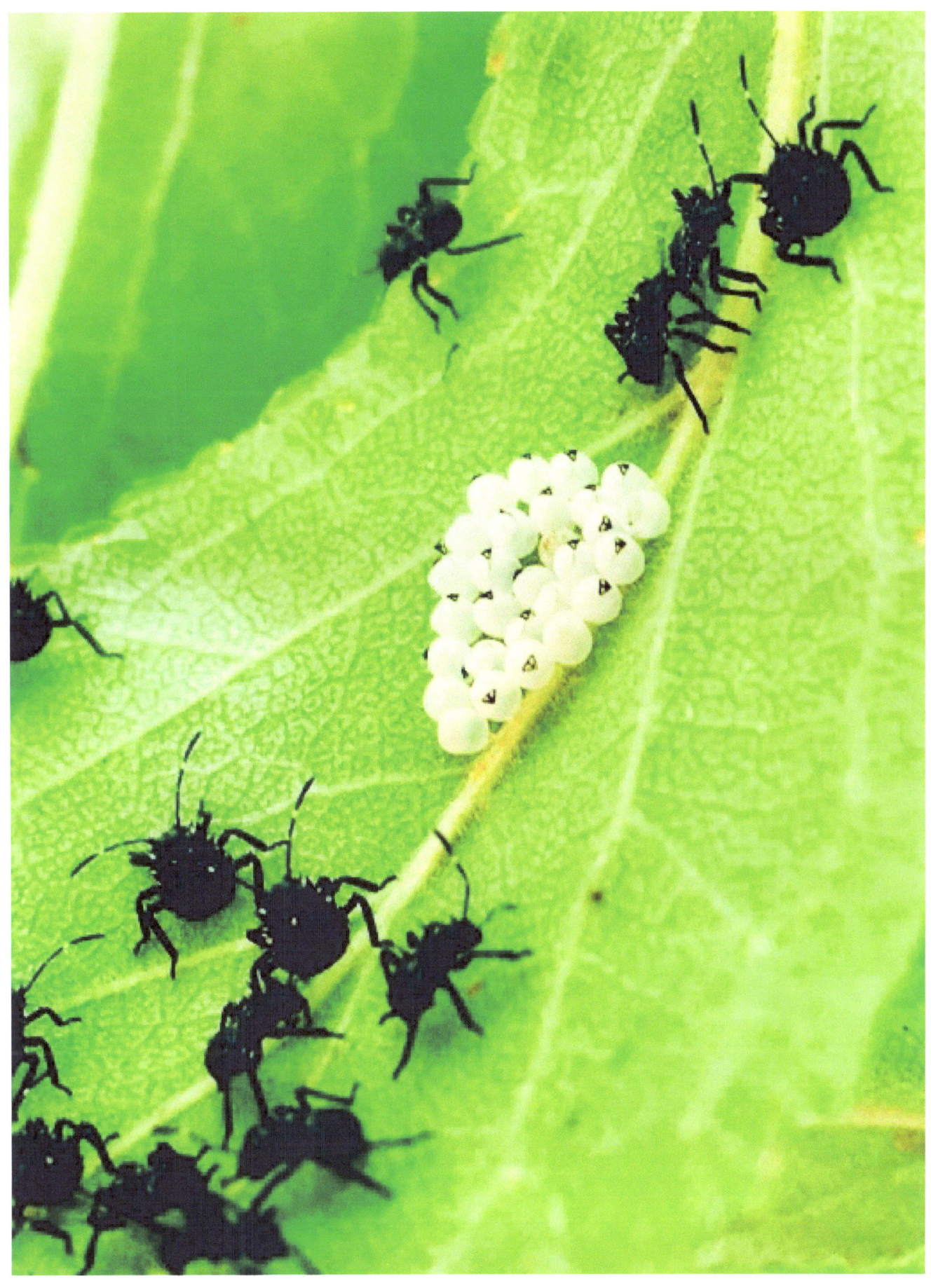

makrōfəˈtägrəfē                                                                                          macrophotography

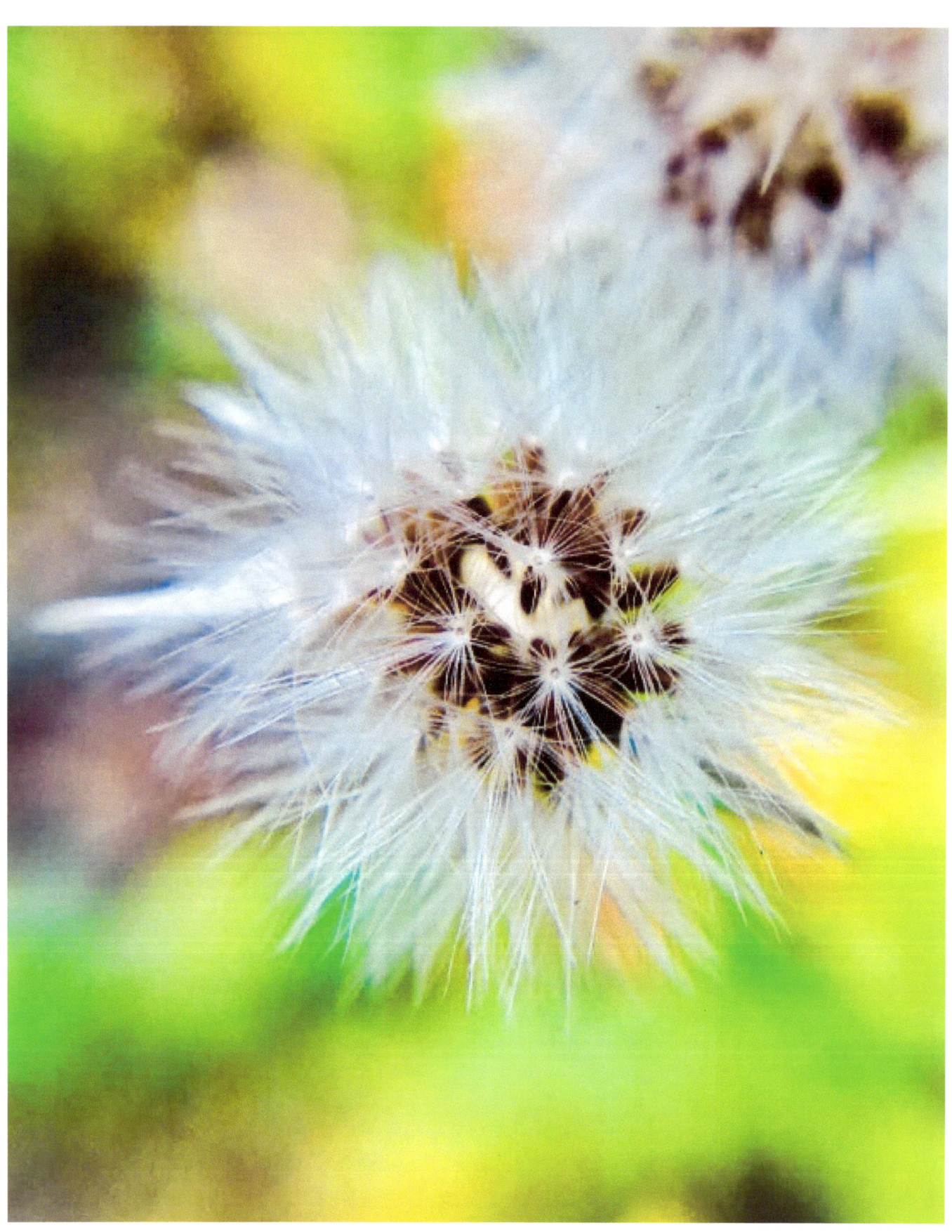

makrōfəˈtägrəfē · macrophotography

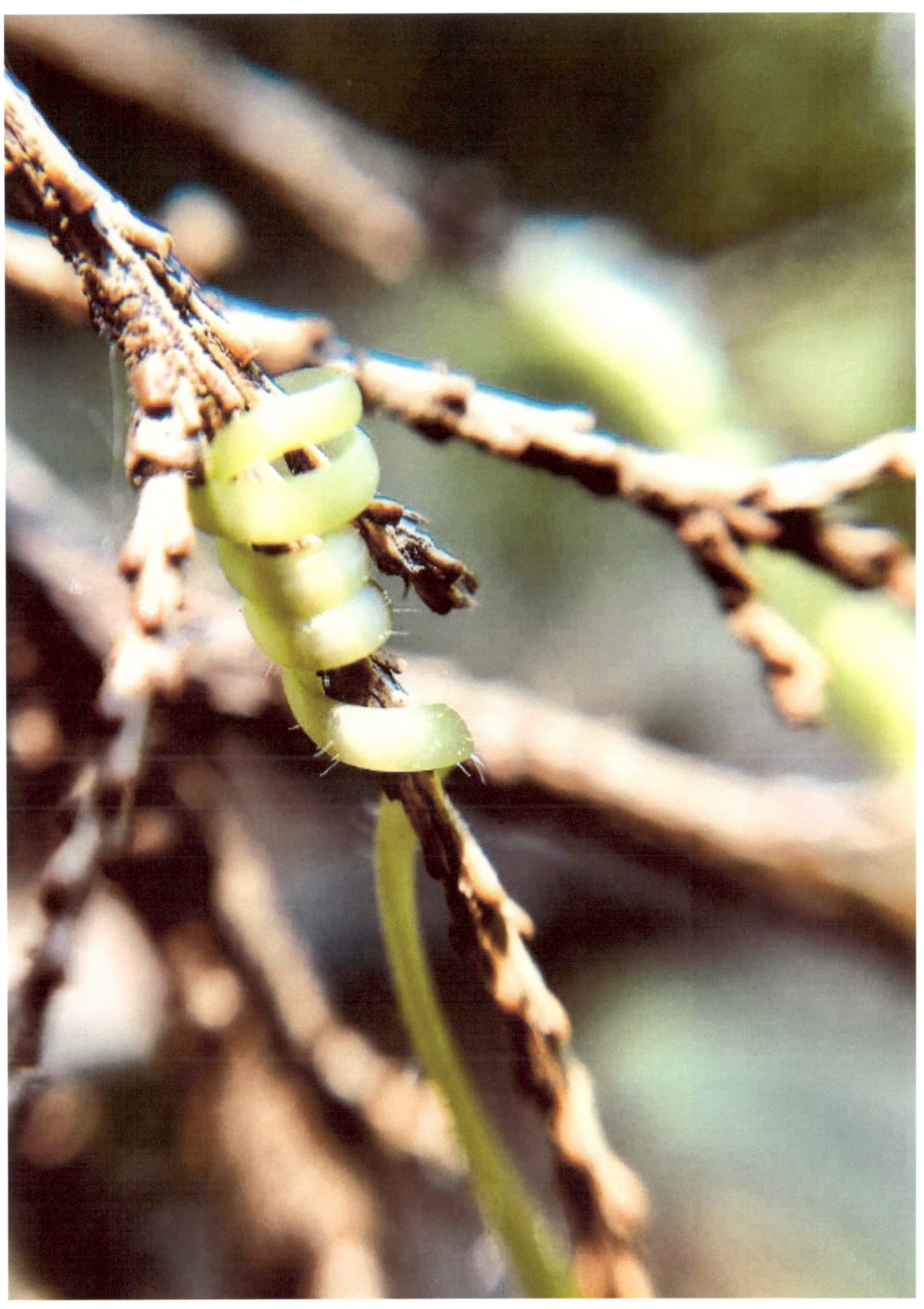

makrōfəˈtägrəfē　　　　　　　　　　　　　　　　　　　　　　　　　　　macrophotography

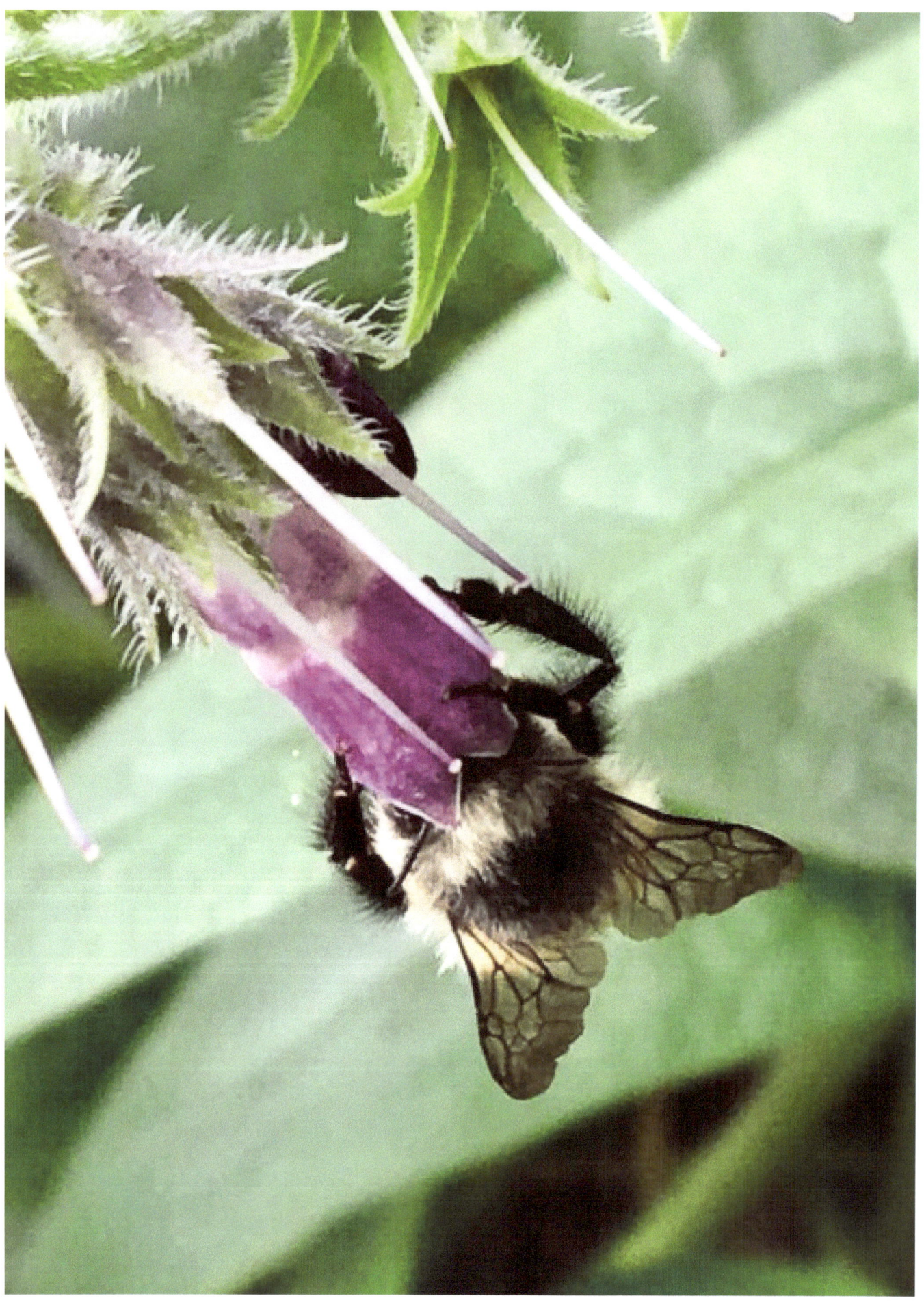

makrōfəˈtägrəfē · macrophotography

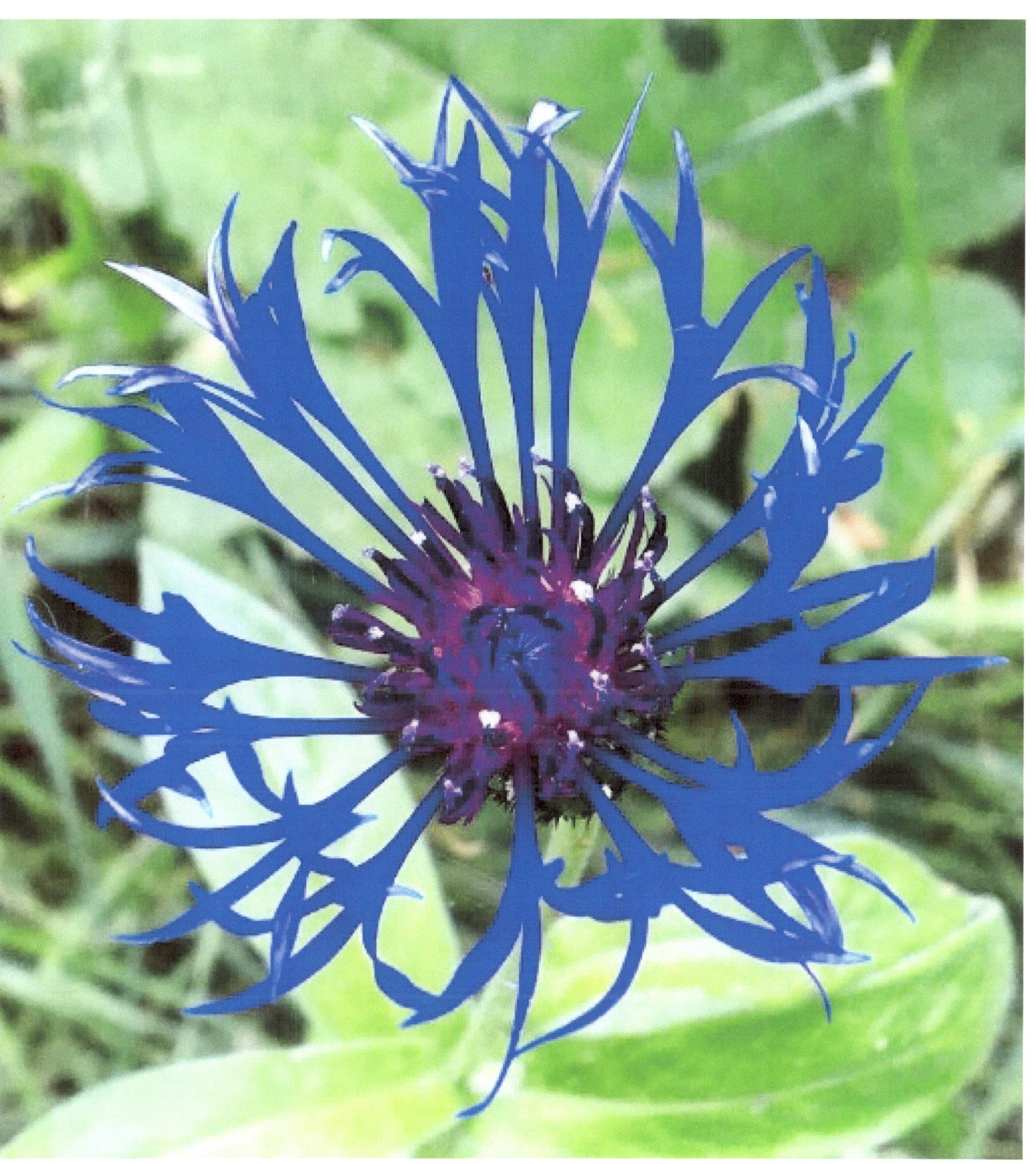

makrōfəˈtägrəfē                                                                                                                              macrophotography

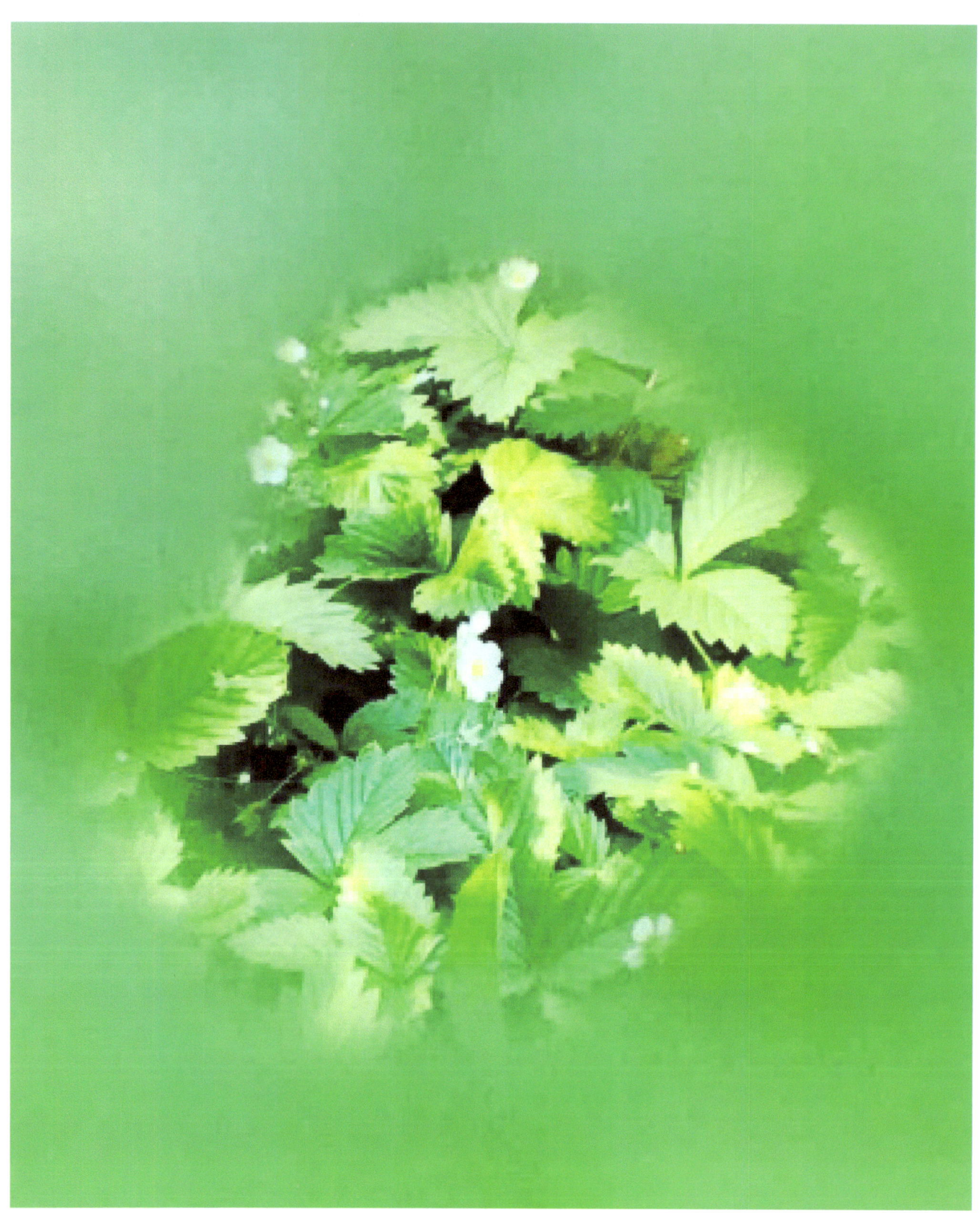

makrōfəˈtägrəfē · macrophotography

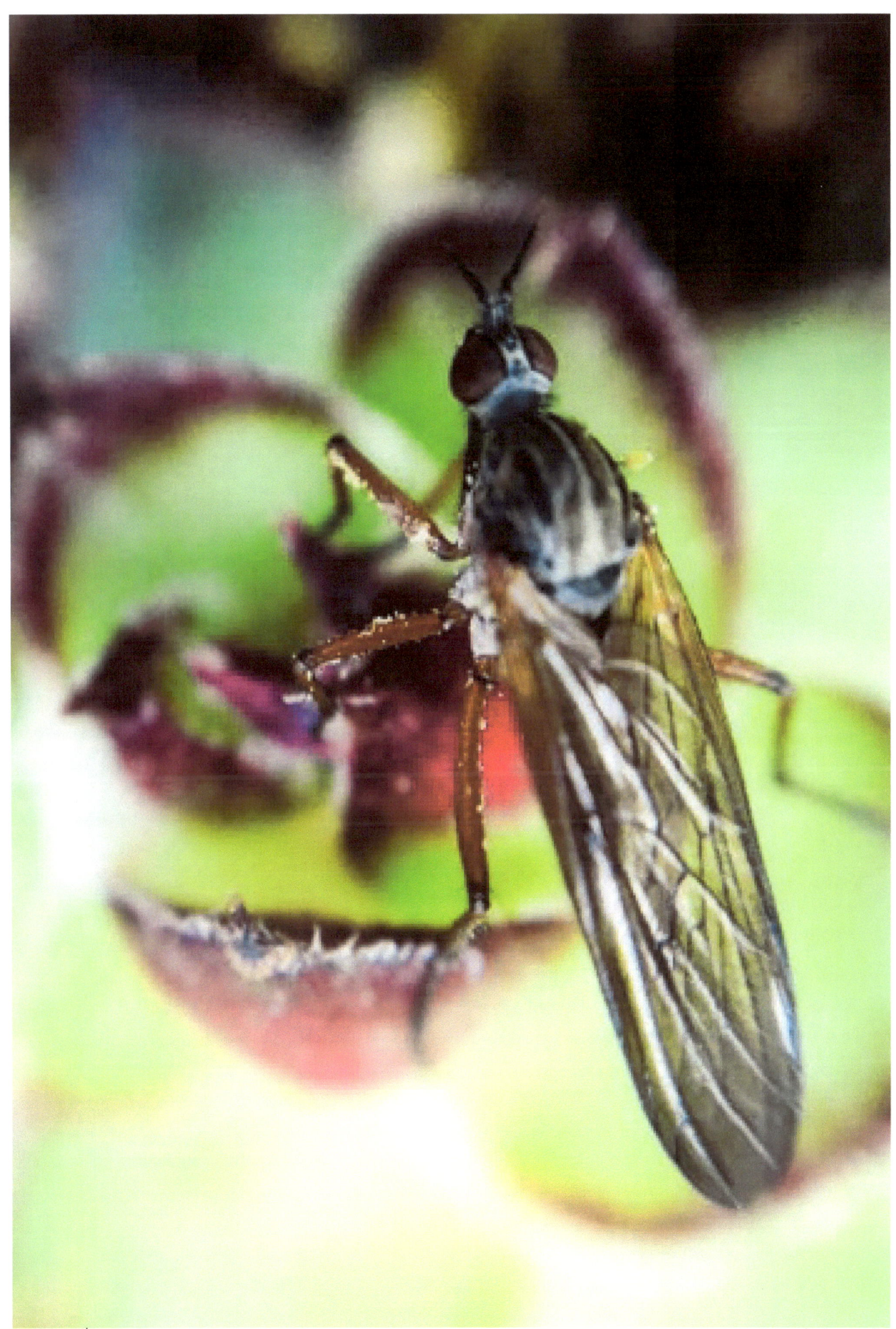

makrōfəˈtägrəfē macrophotography

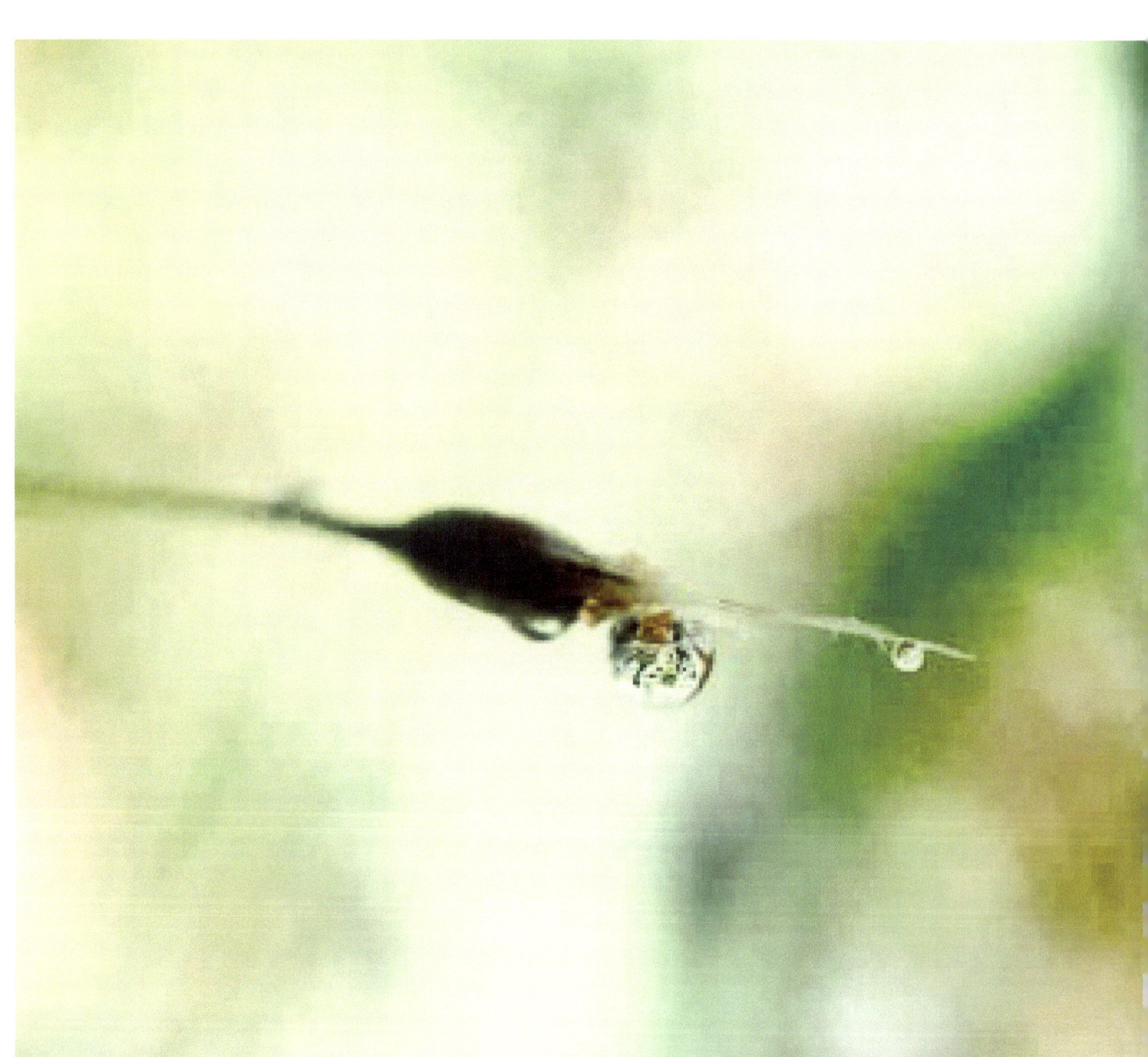

makrōfəˈtägrəfē   macrophotography

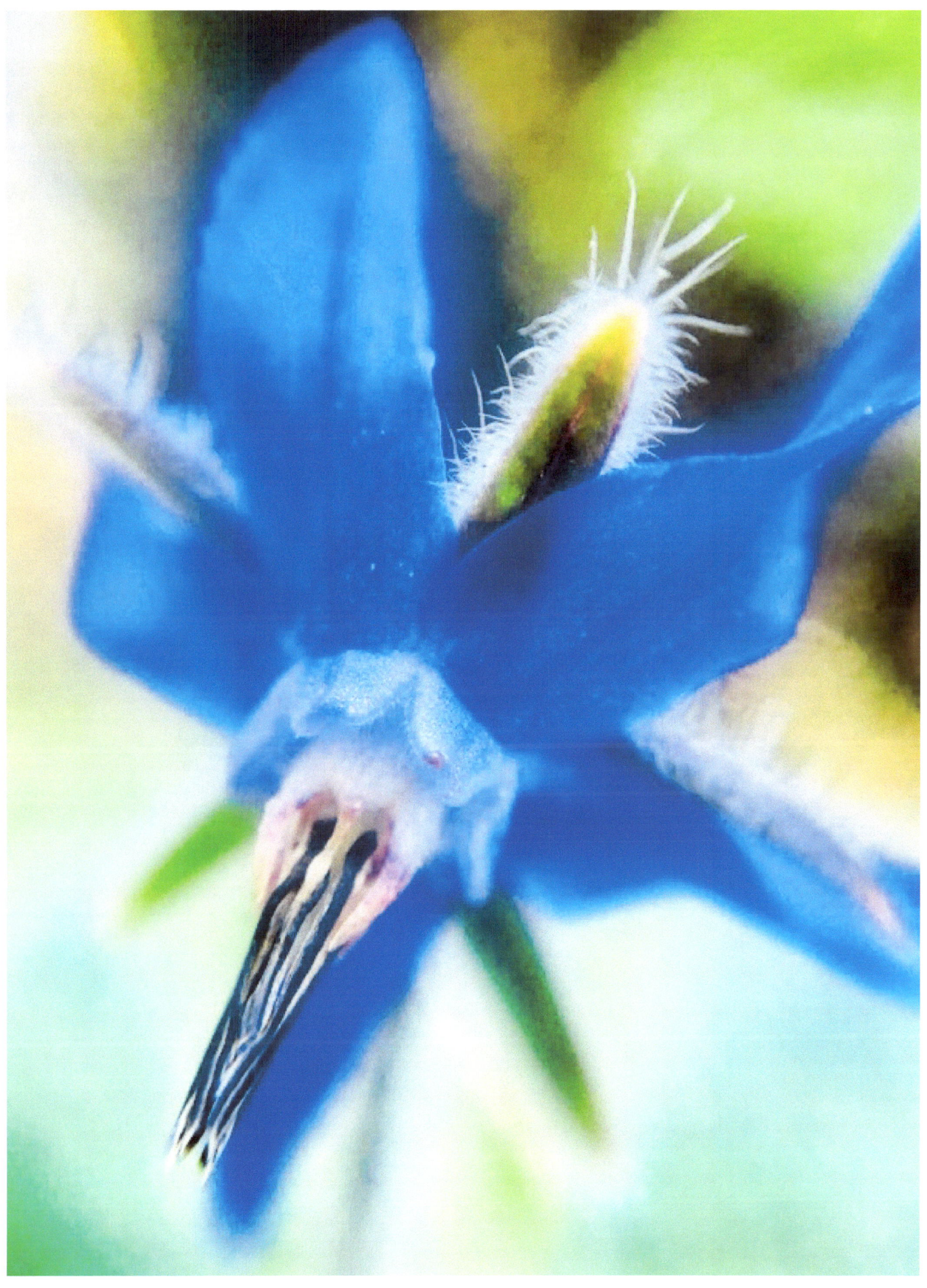

makrōfəˈtägrəfē						macrophotography

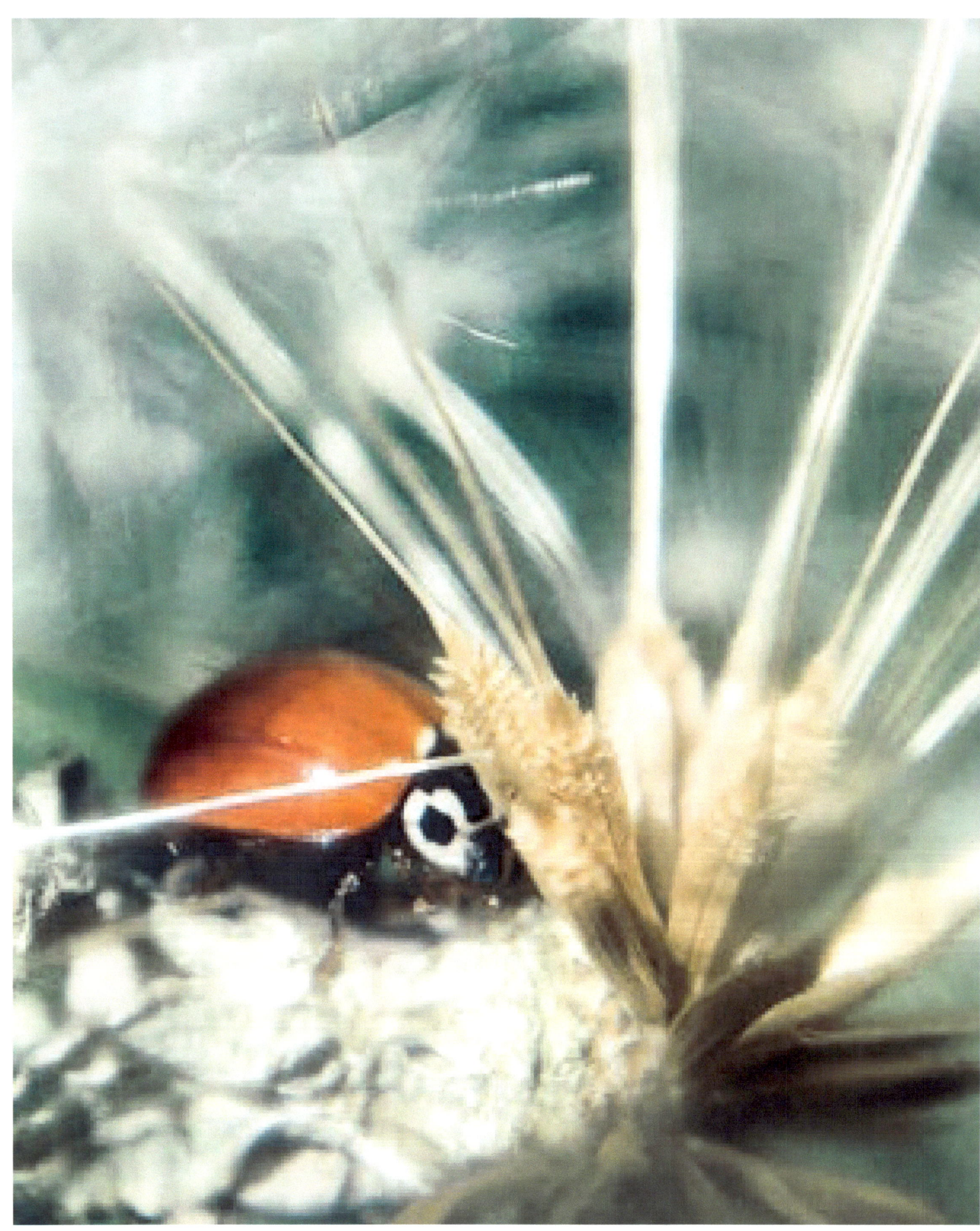

makrōfəˈtägrəfē — macrophotography

makrōfəˈtägrəfē 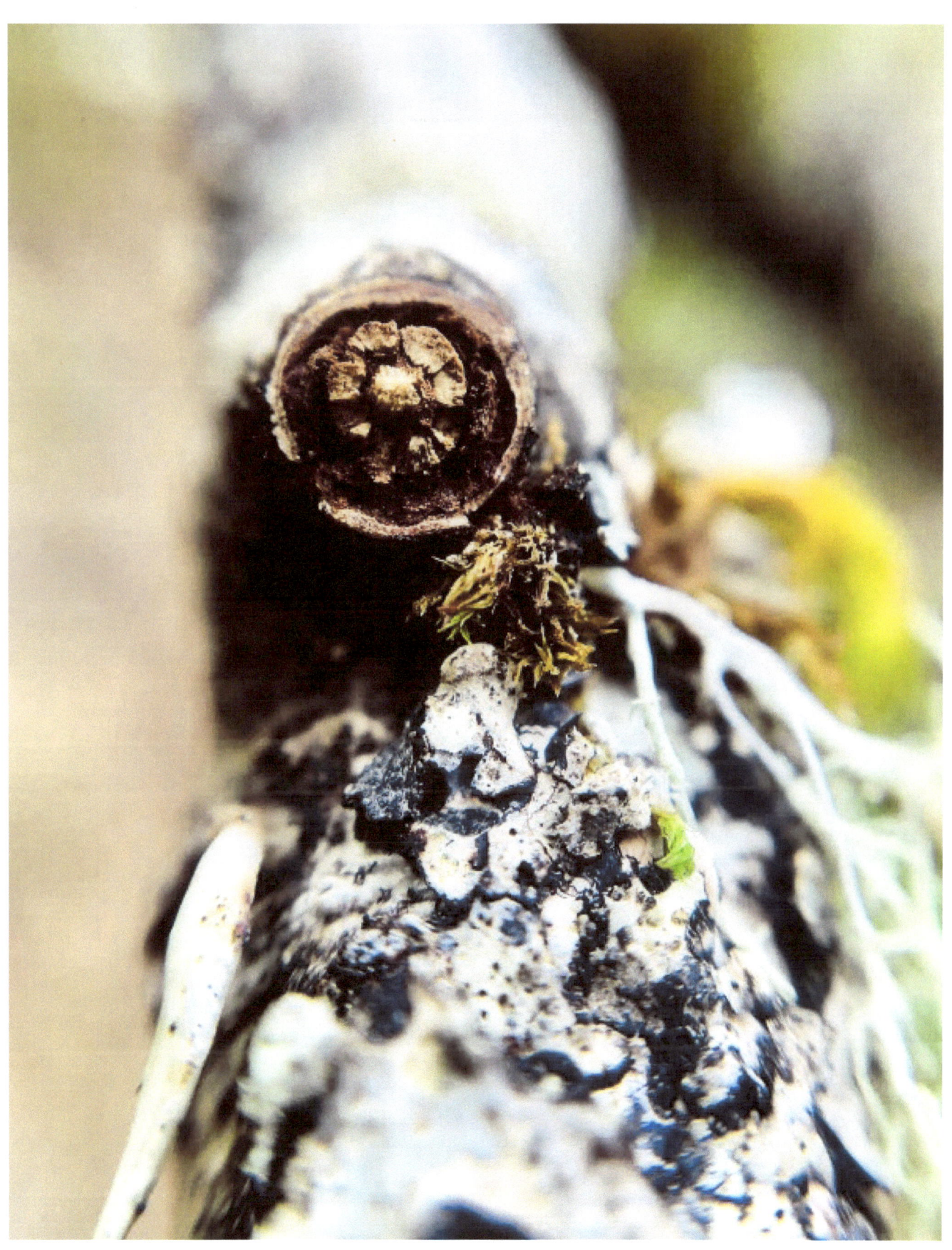 macrophotography

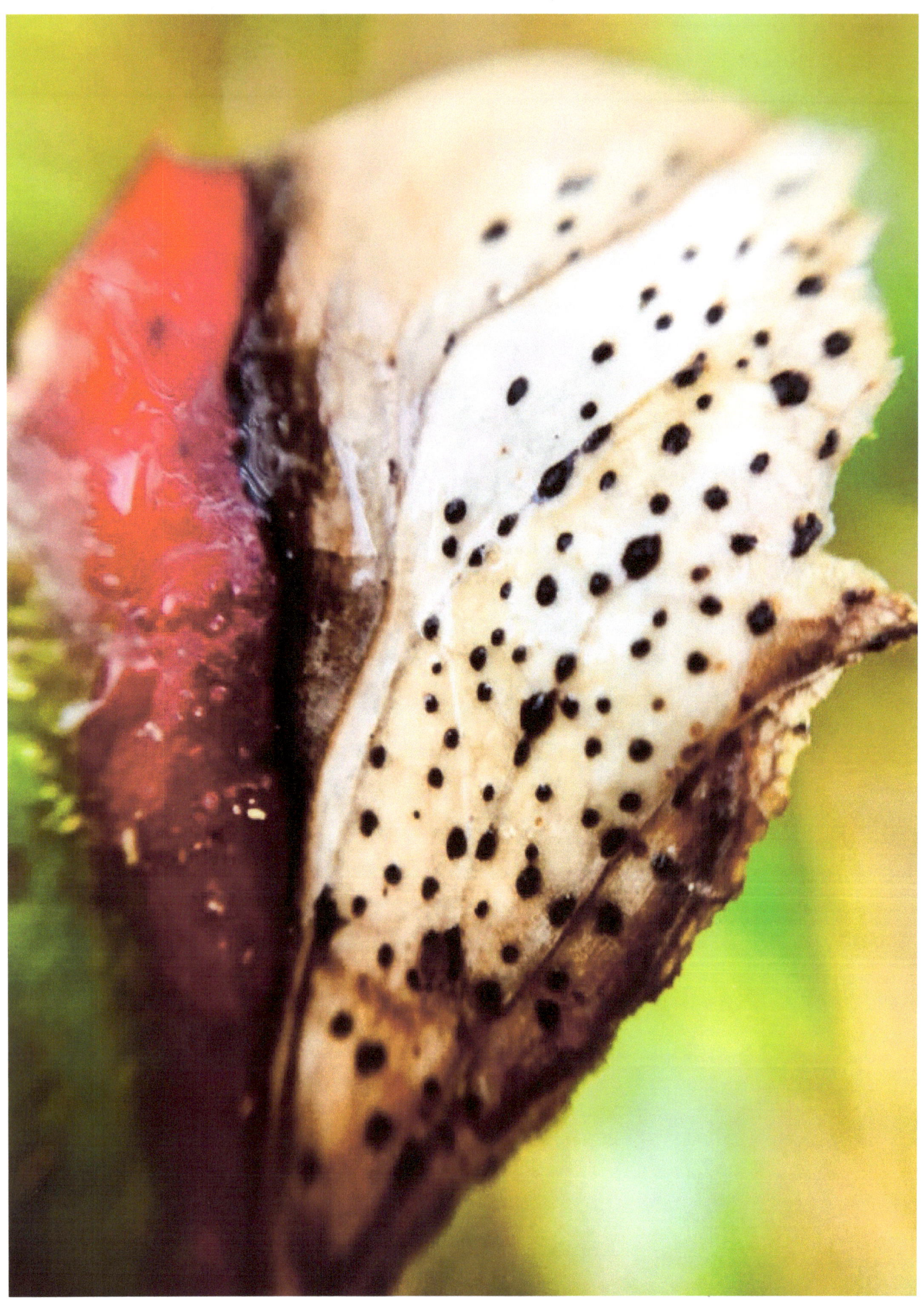

makrōfəˈtägrəfē     macrophotography

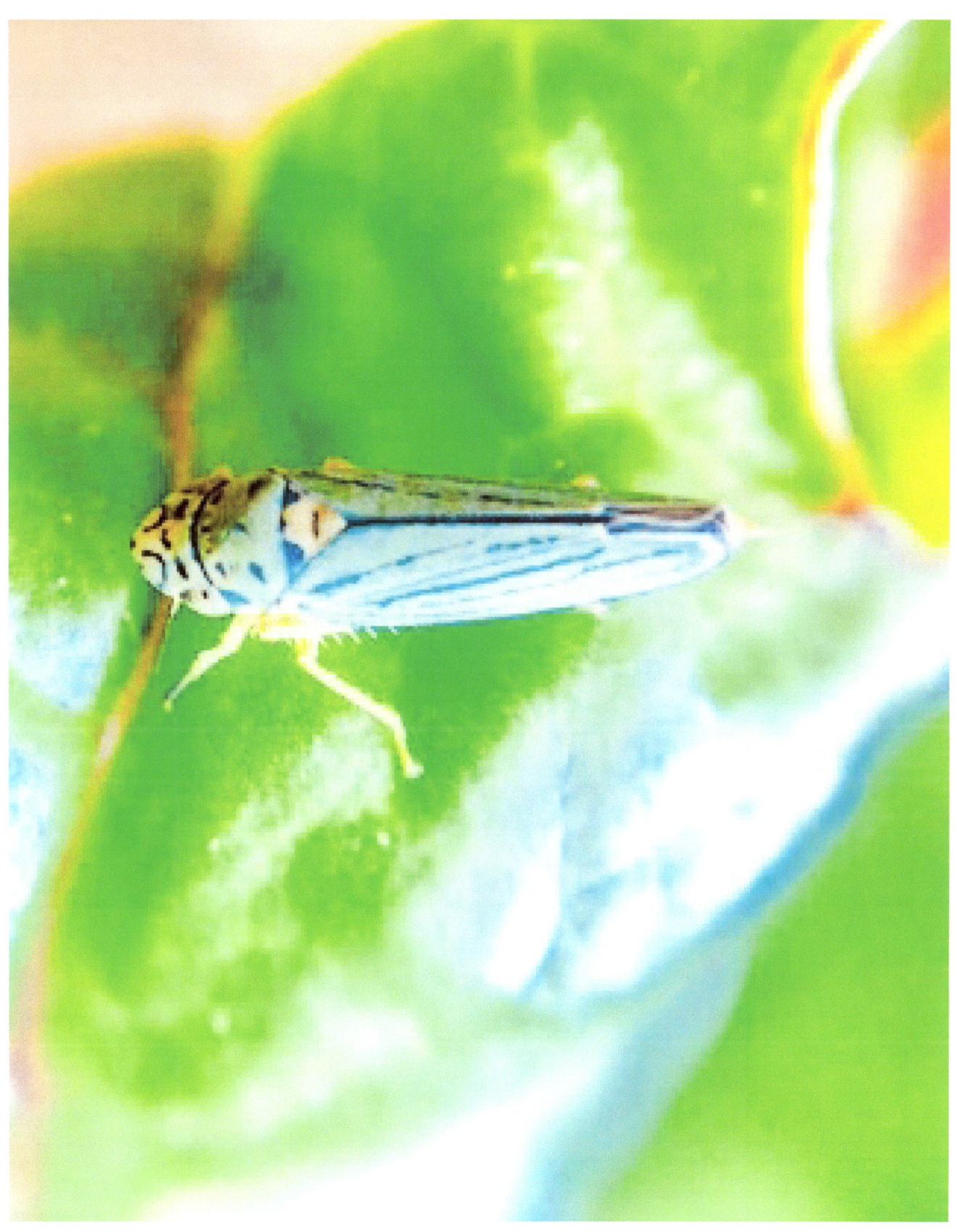

makrōfəˈtägrəfē                                                              macrophotography

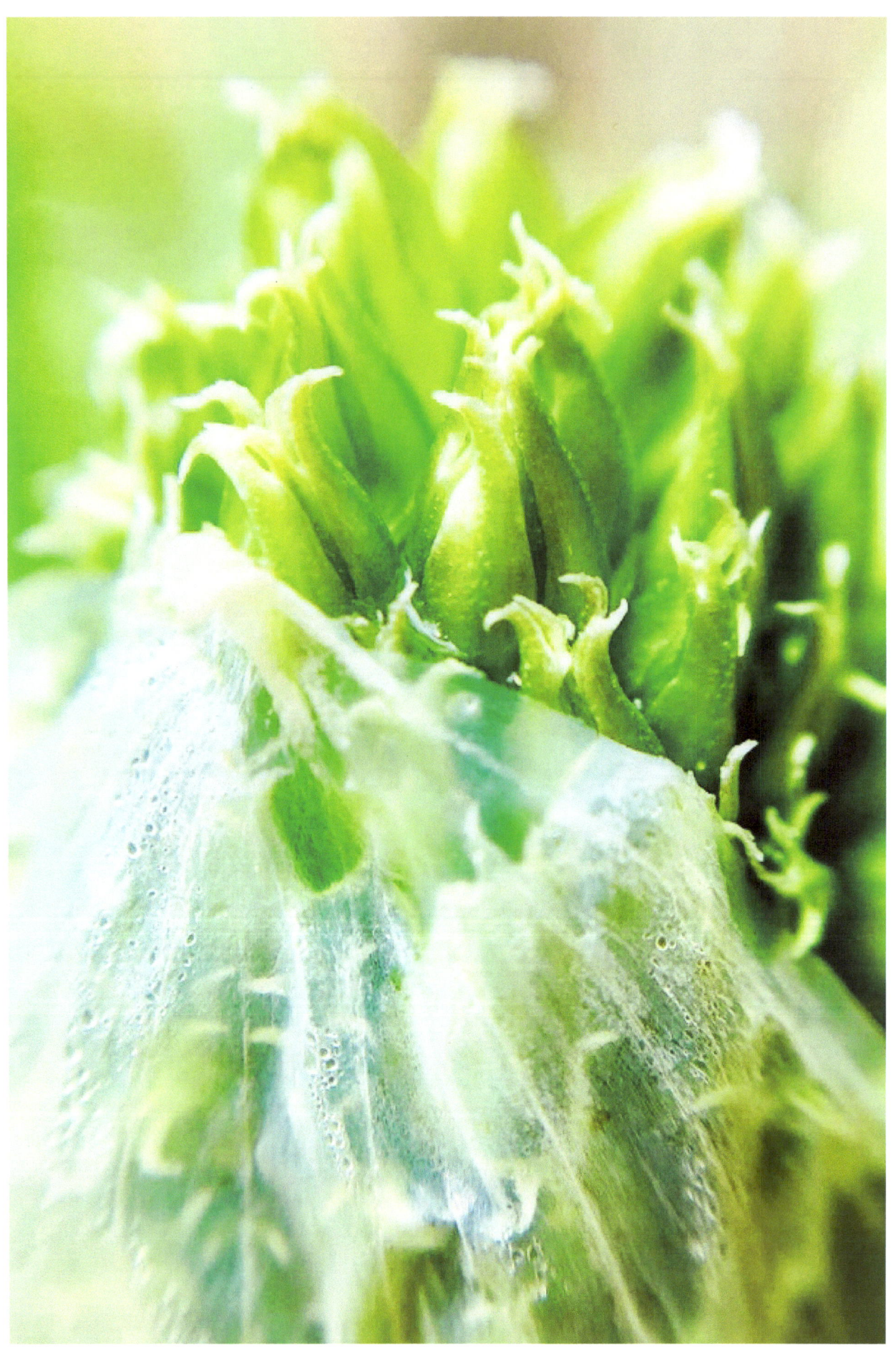

makrōfəˈtägrəfē macrophotography

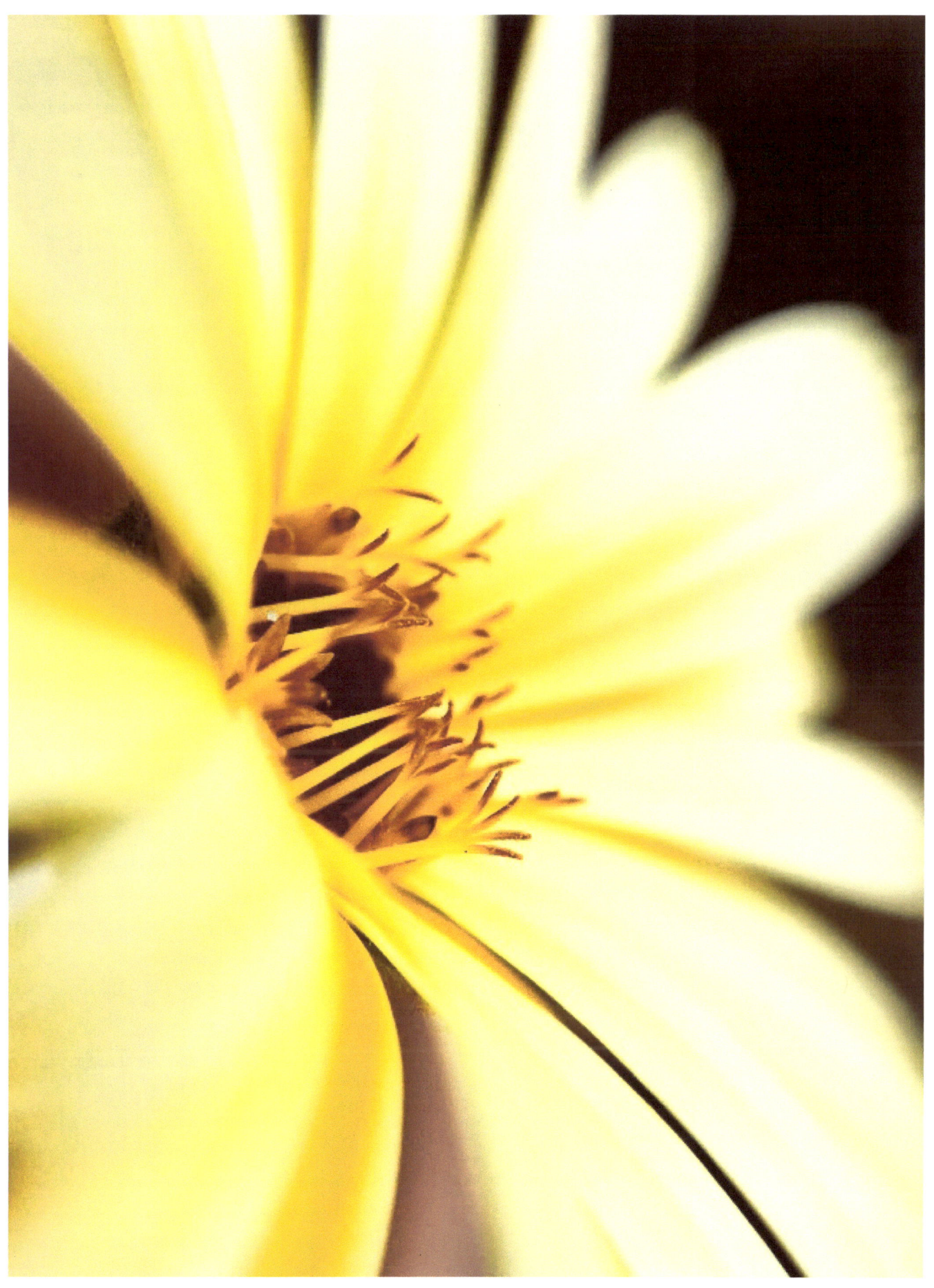

makrōfə'tägrəfē        macrophotography

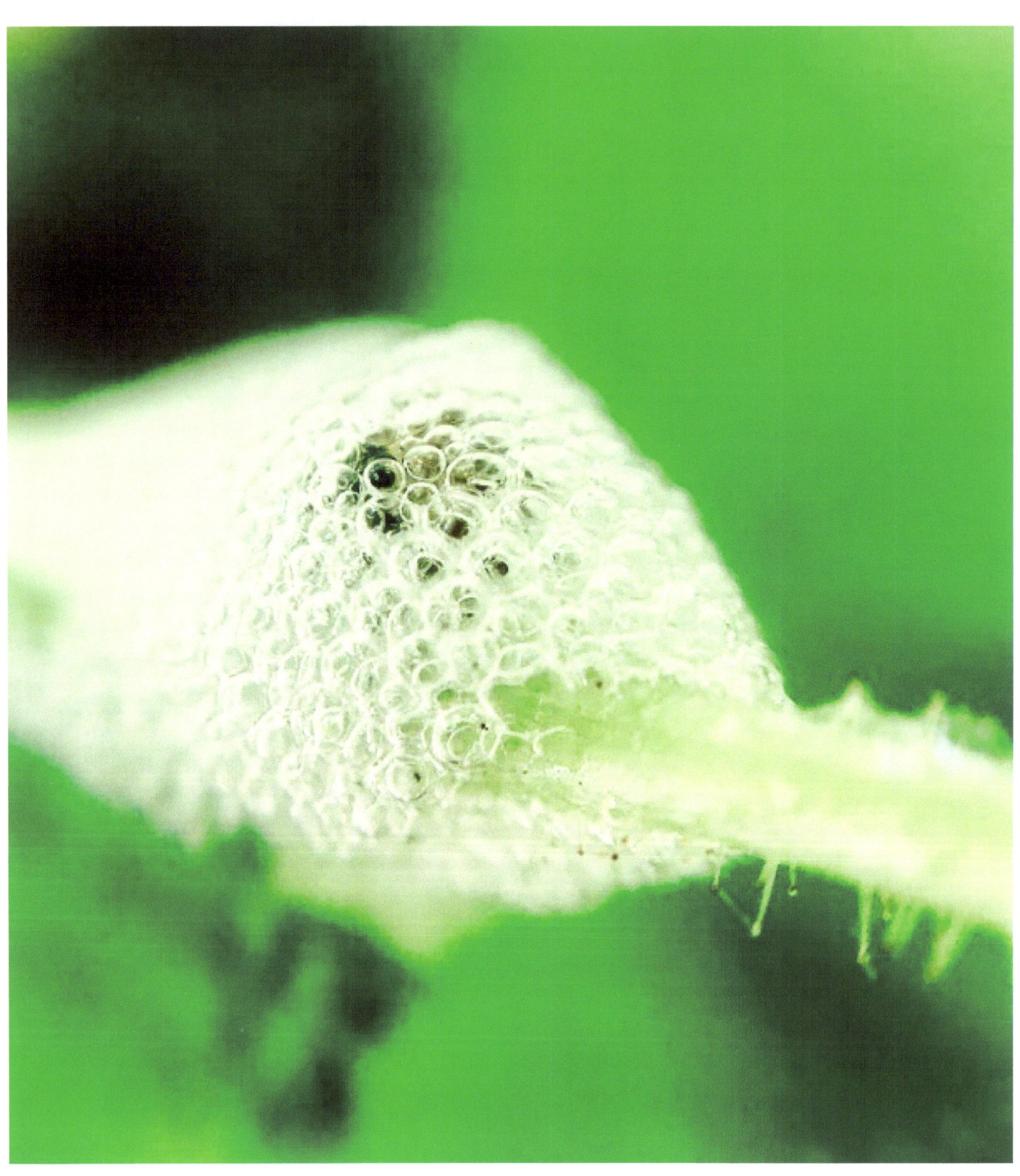

makrōfə'tägrəfē    macrophotography

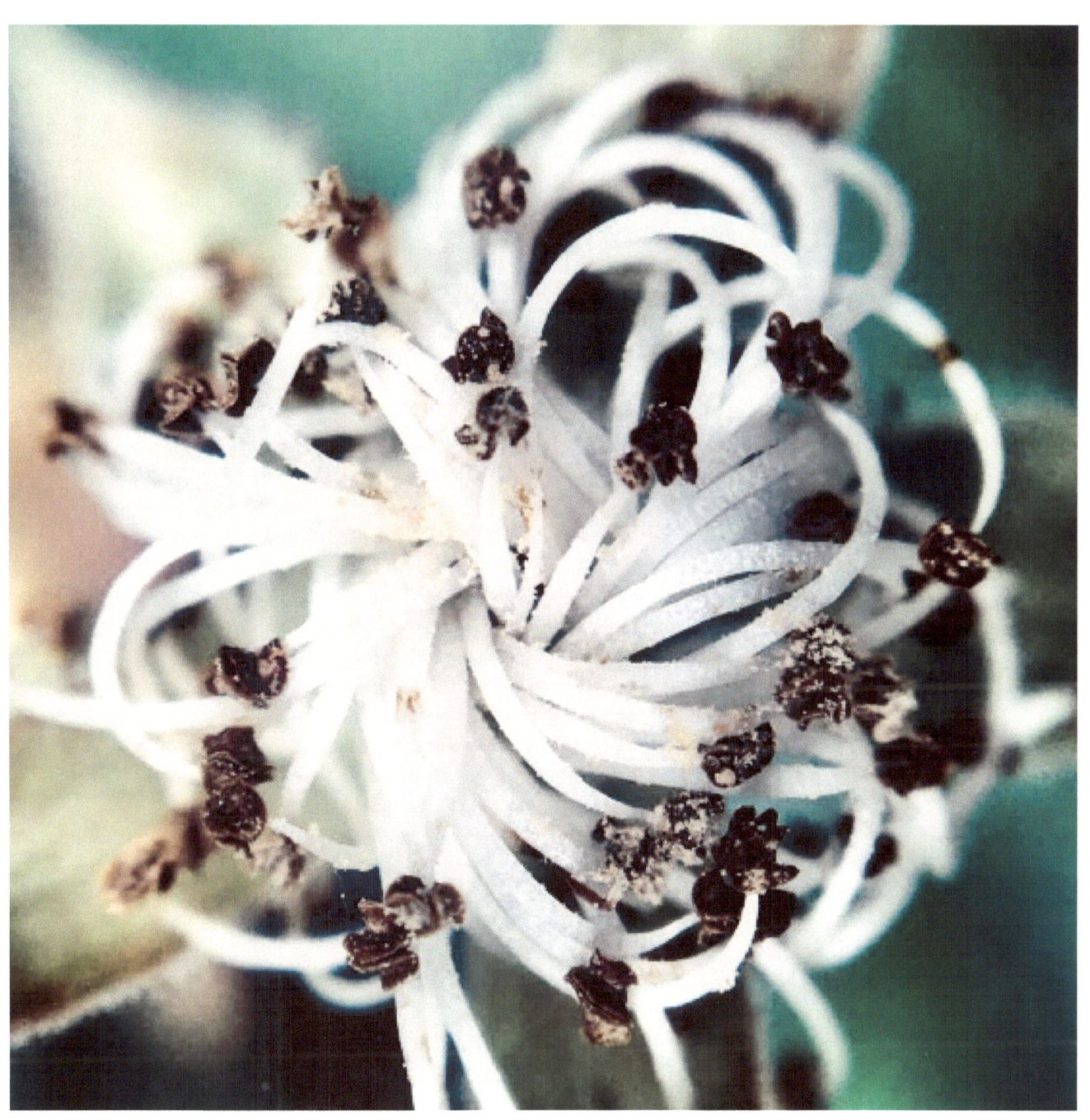

makrōfəˈtägrəfē                                                                                              macrophotography

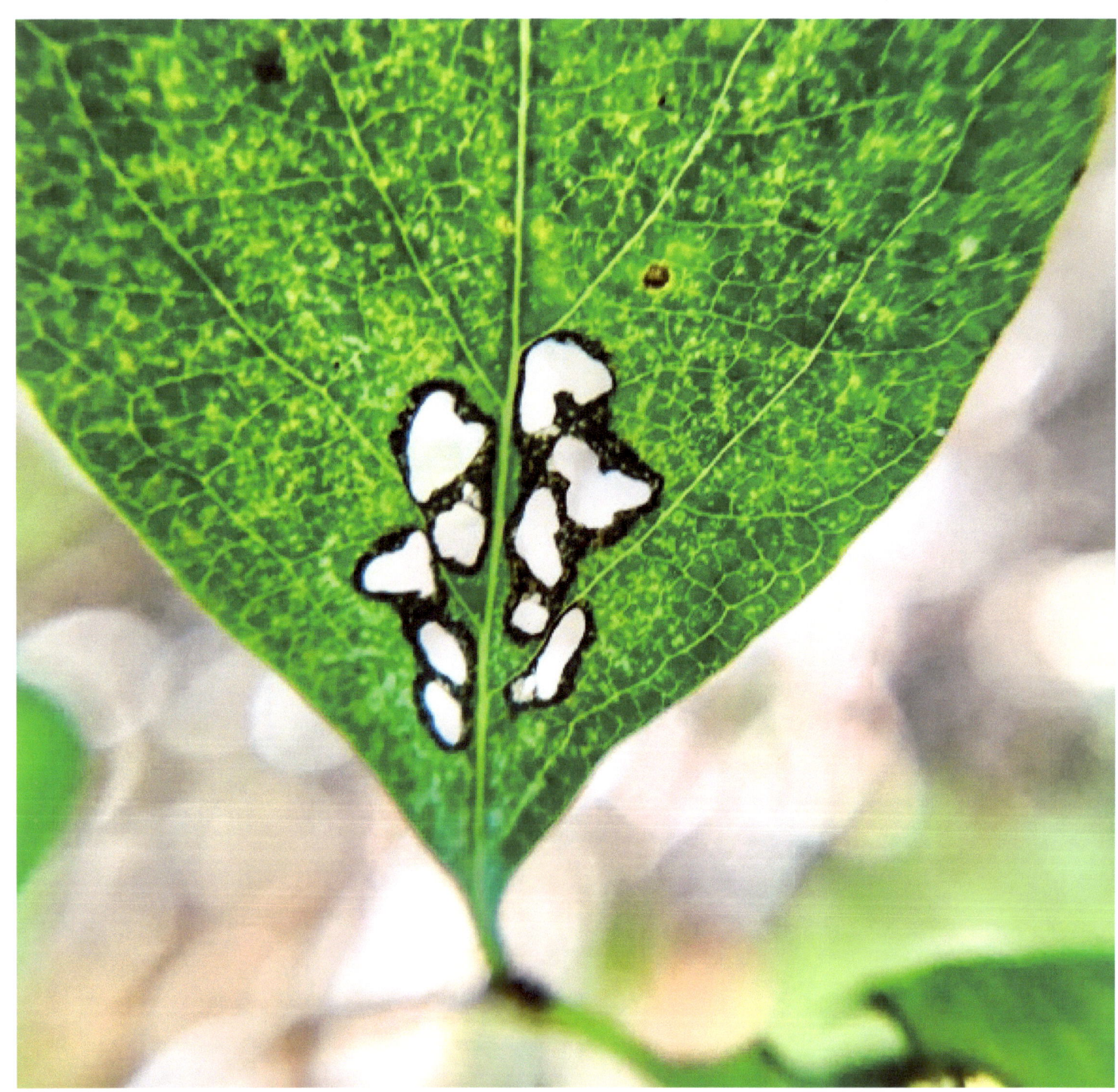

makrōfəˈtägrəfē · macrophotography

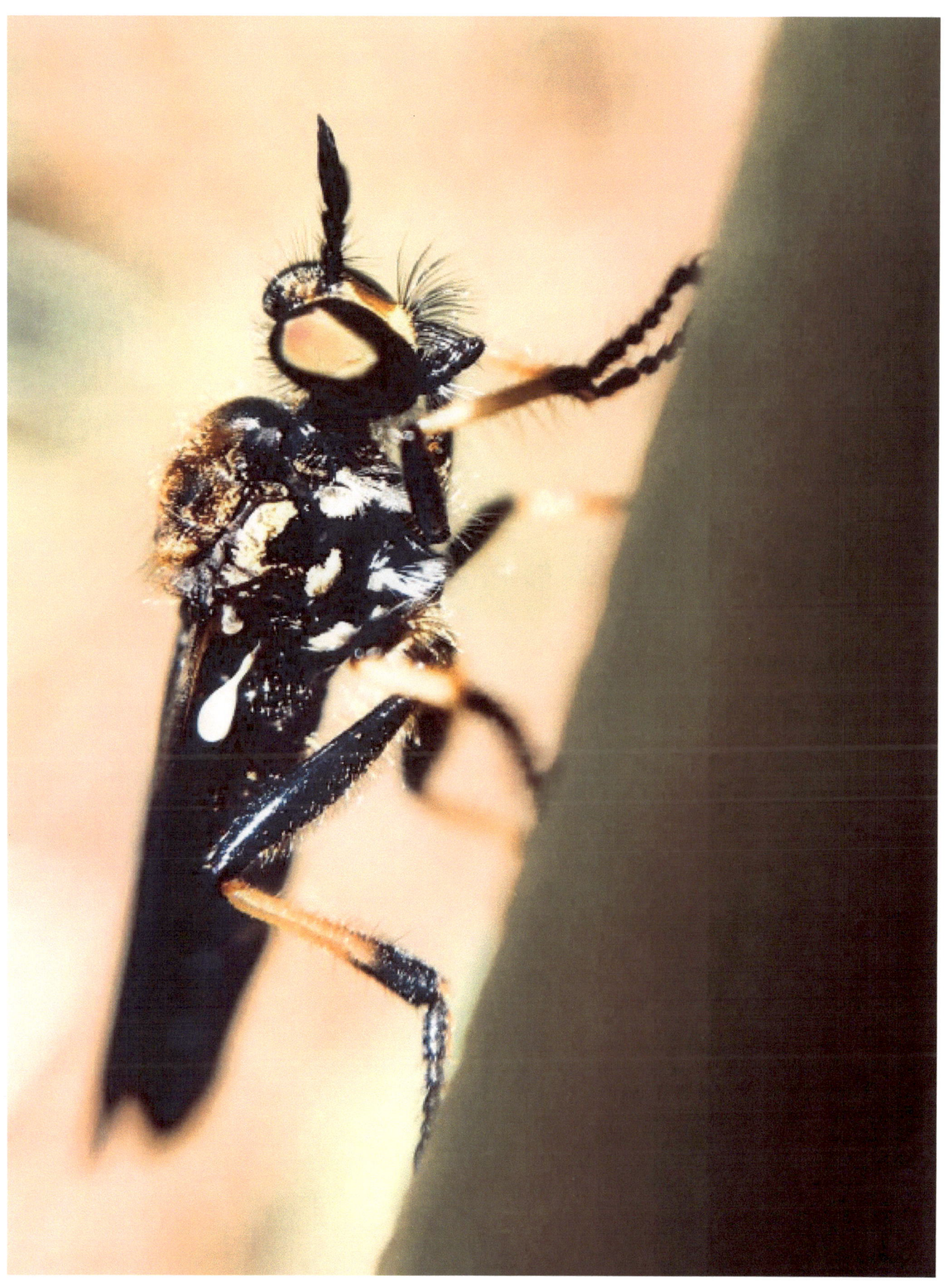

makrōfəˈtägrəfē macrophotography

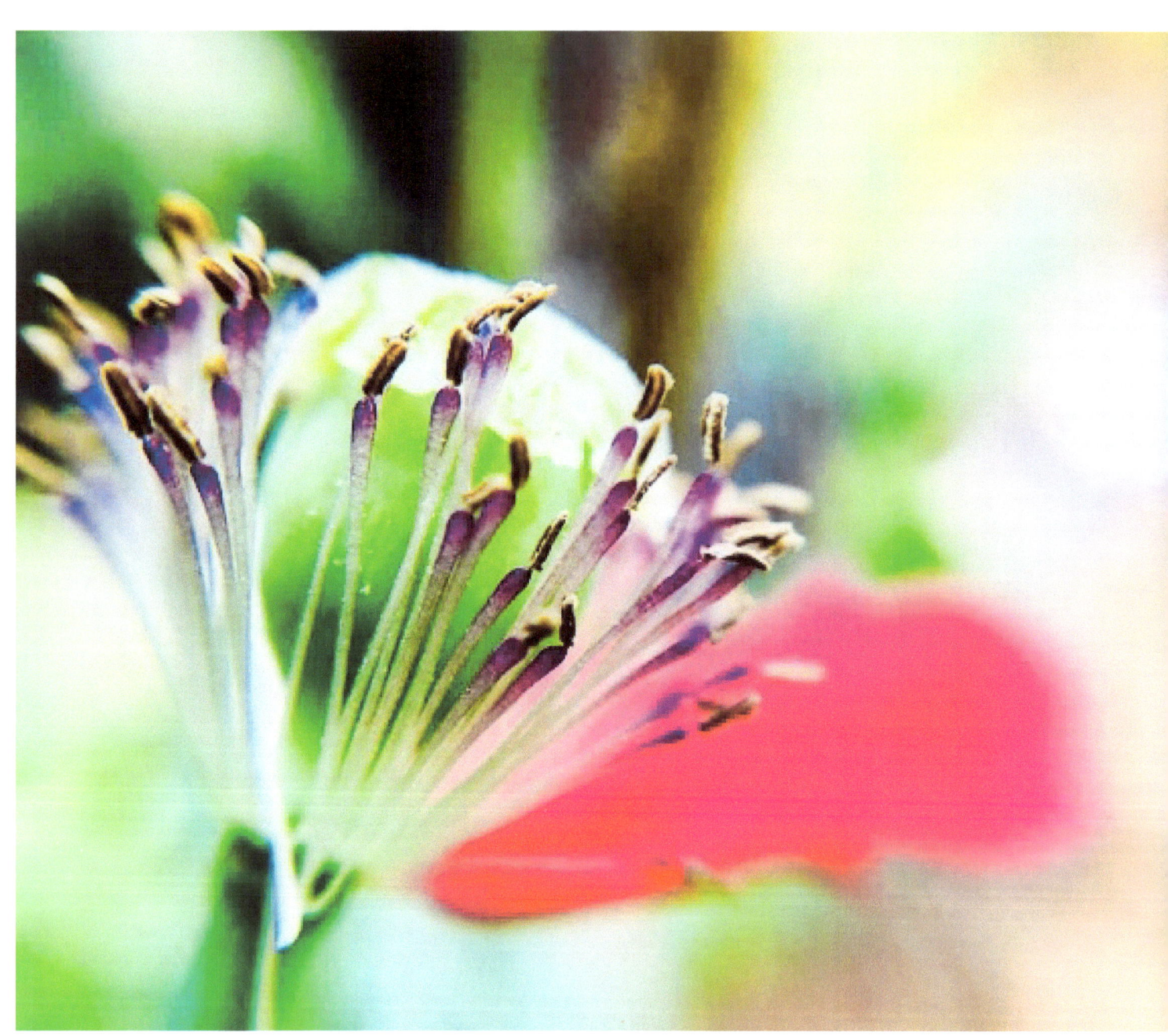

makrōfəˈtägrəfē  macrophotography

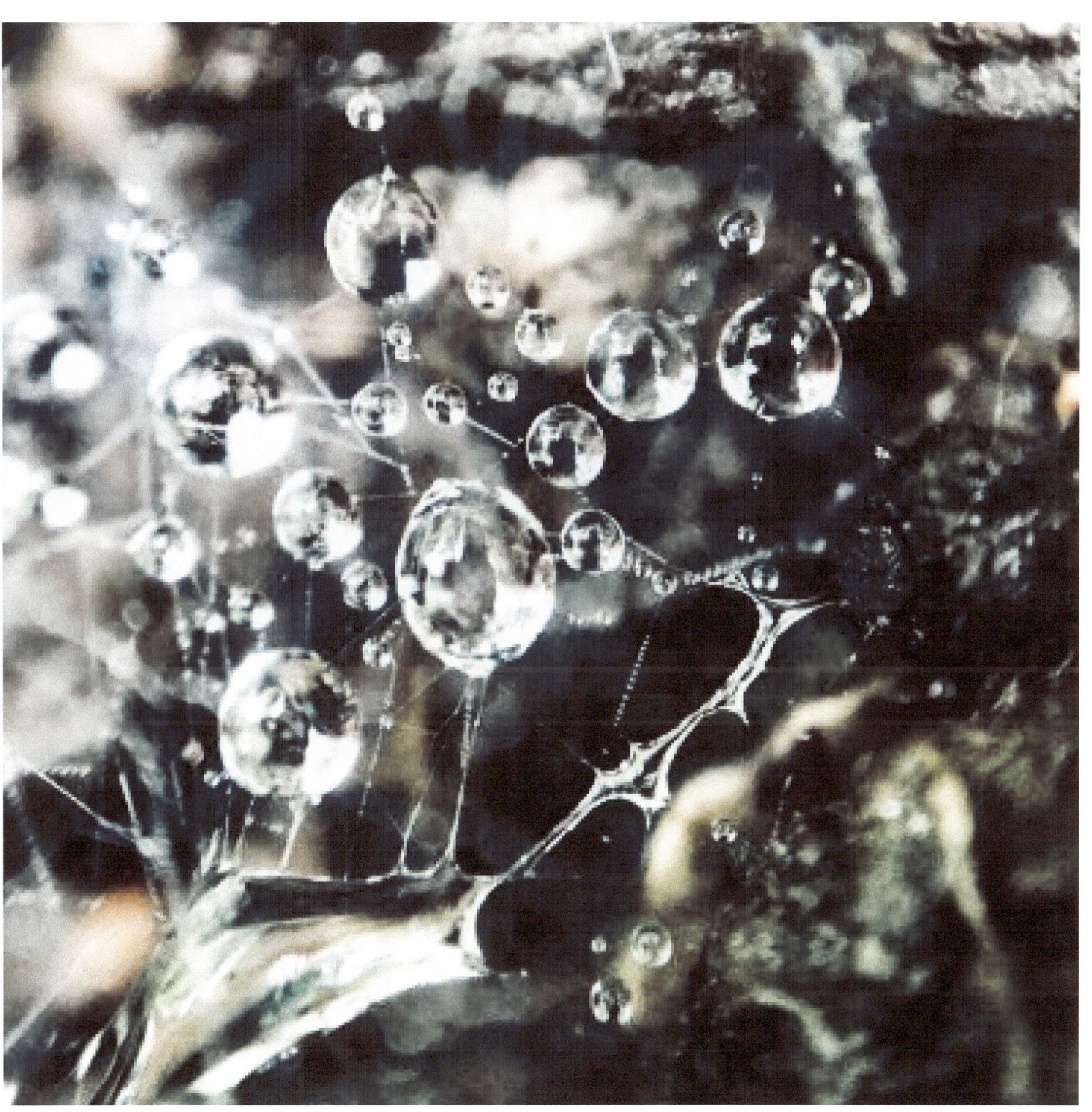

makrōfəˈtägrəfē     macrophotography

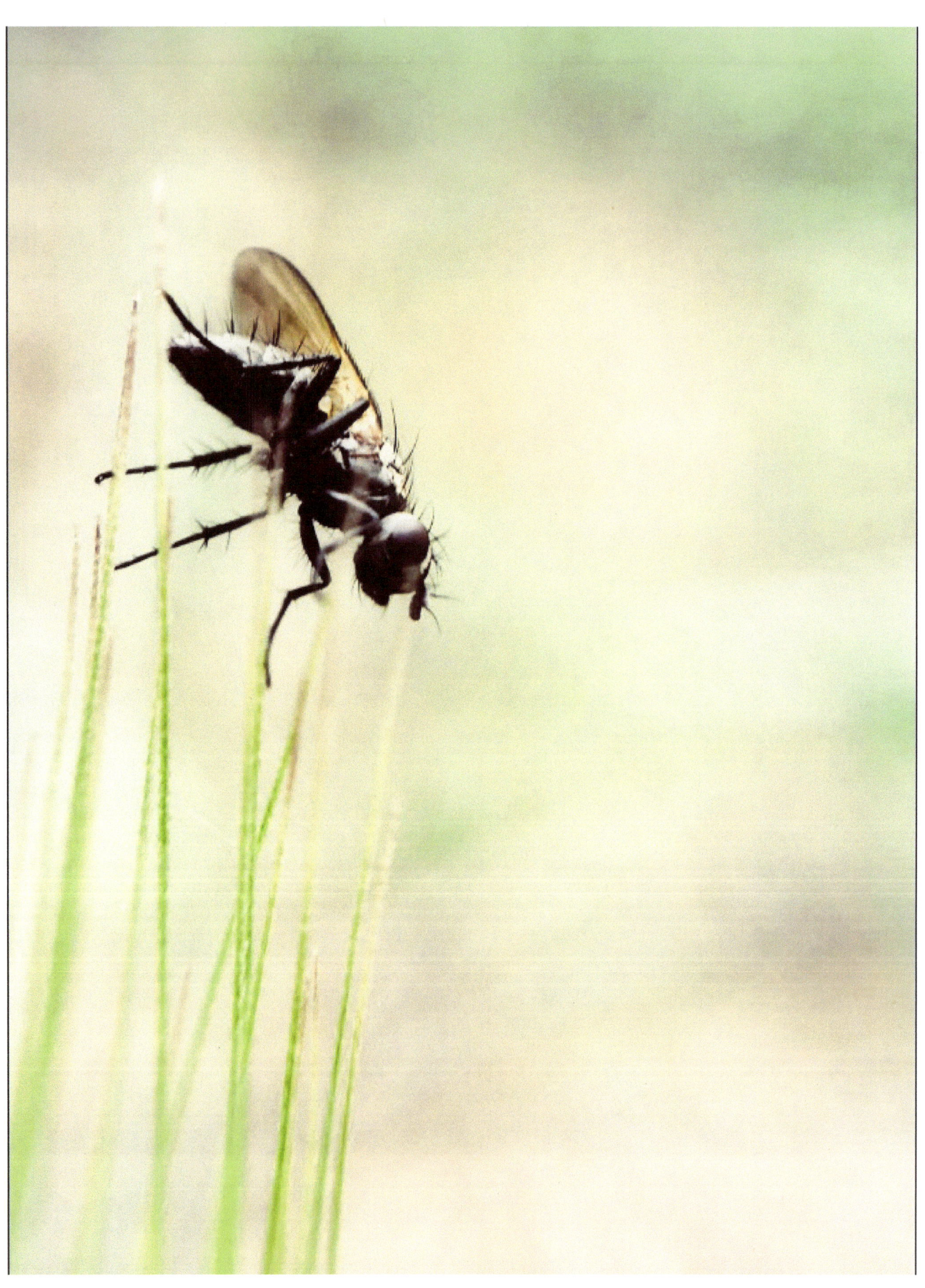

makrōfəˈtägrəfē macrophotography

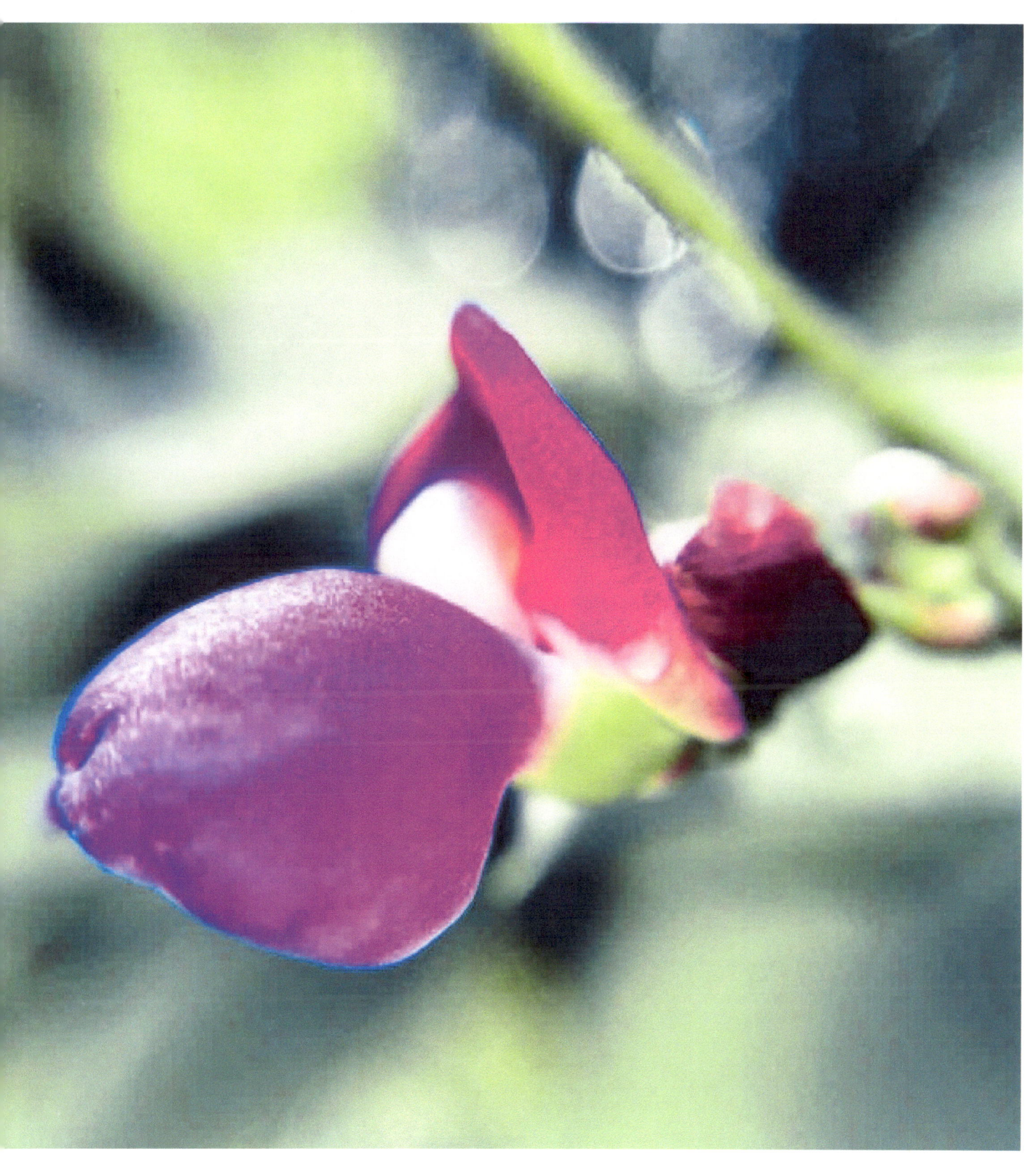

makrōfəˈtägrəfē        macrophotography

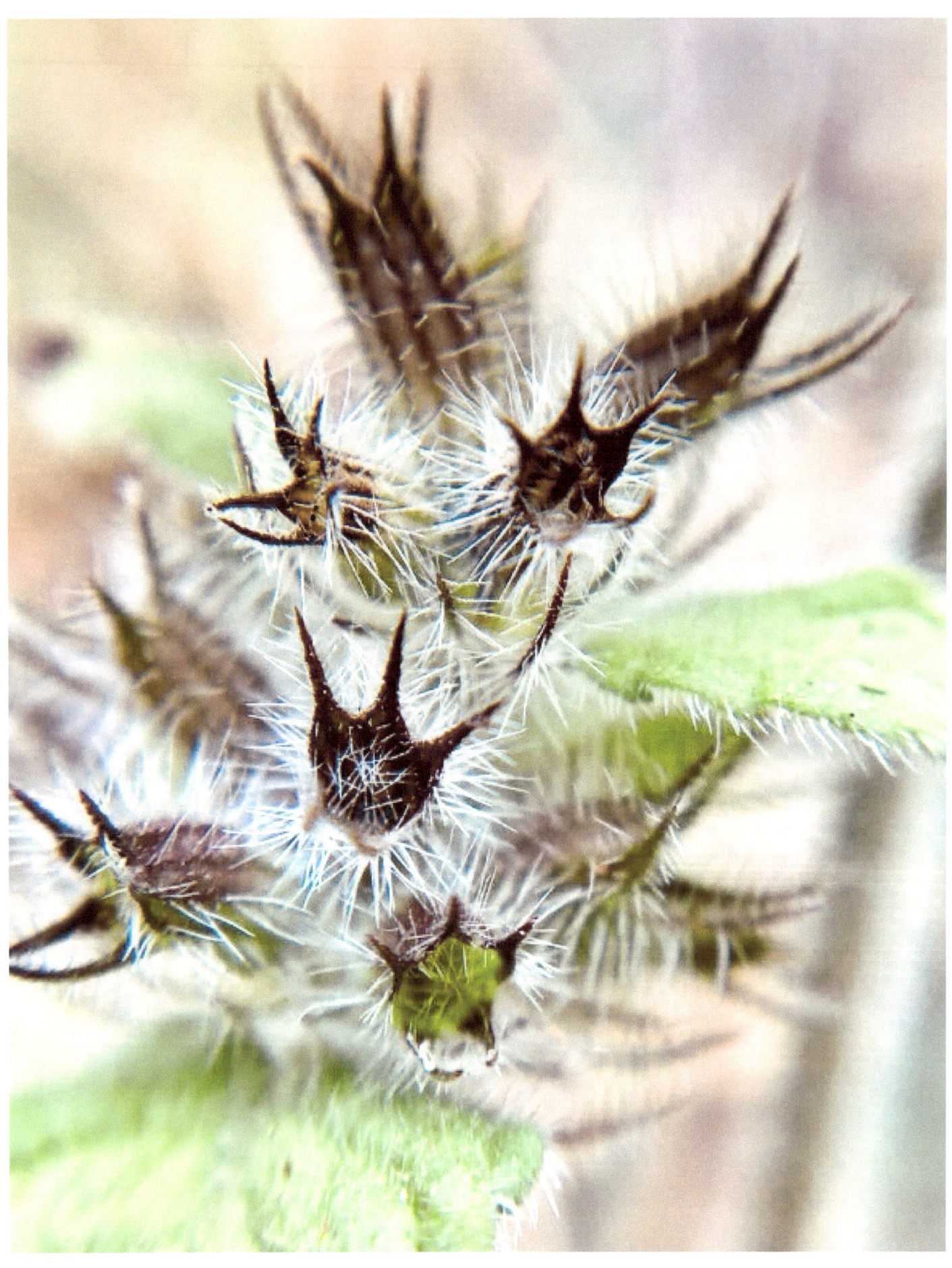

makrōfəˈtägrəfē                                                                                              macrophotography

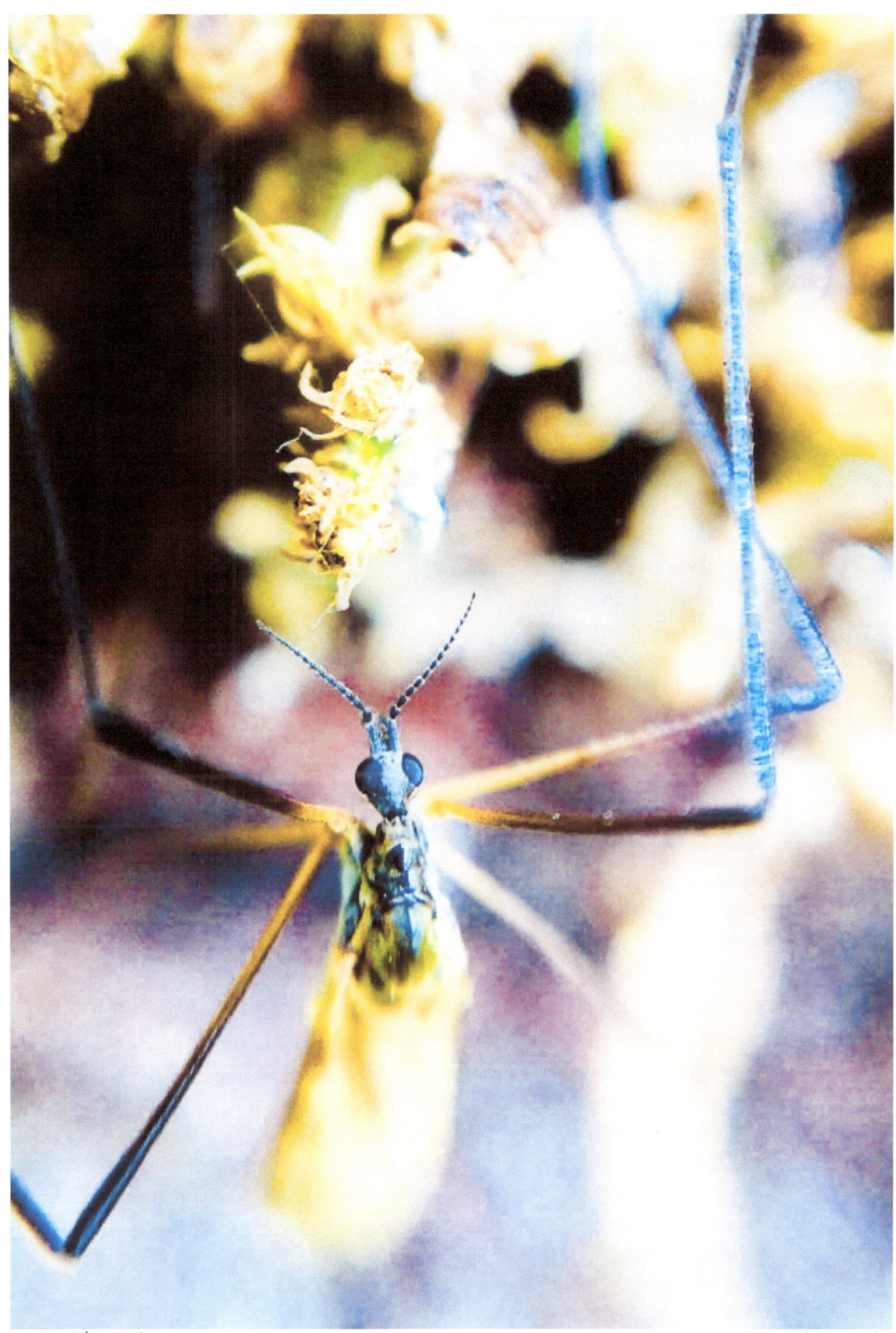

makrōfəˈtägrəfē macrophotography

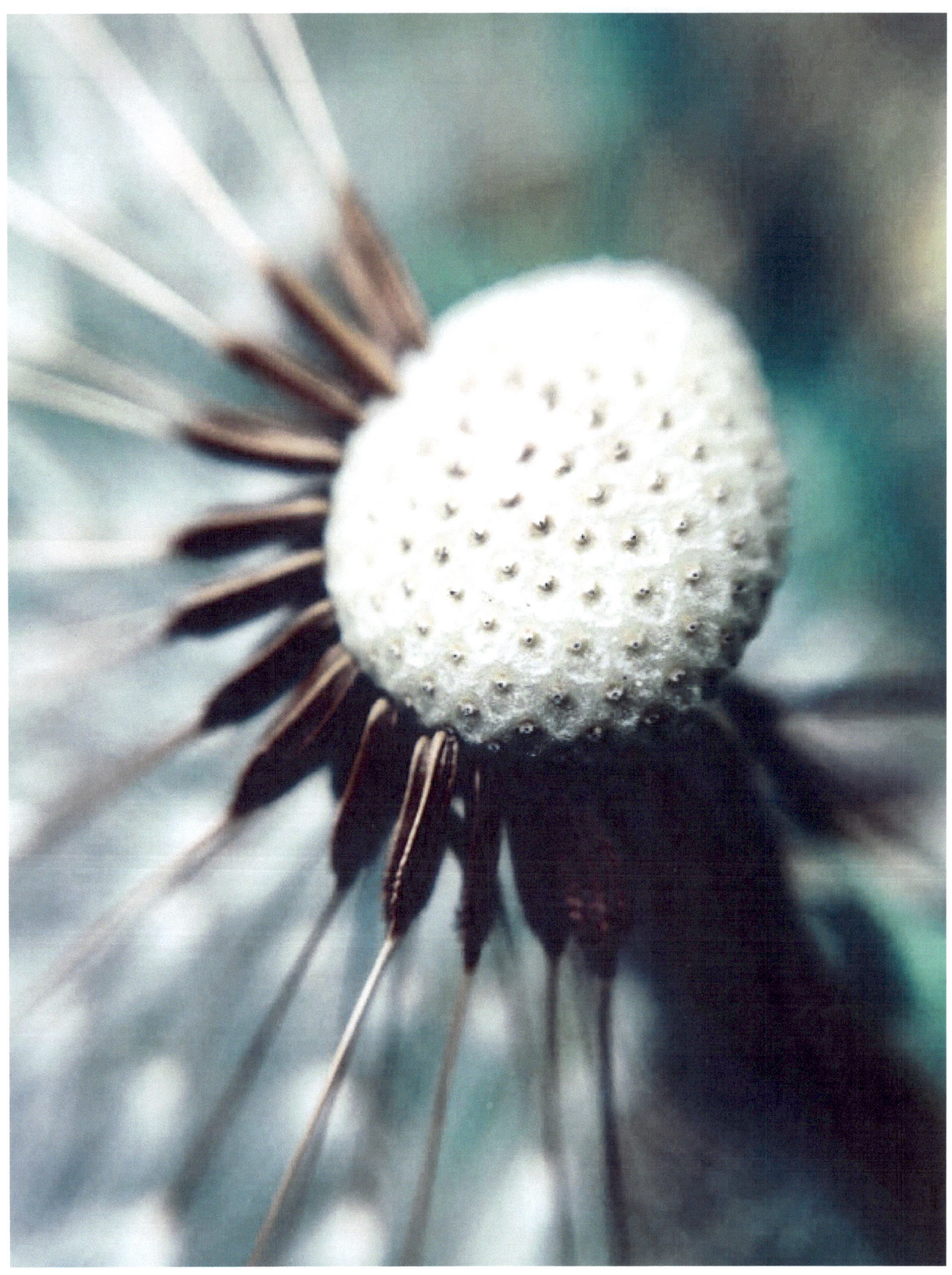

makrōfəˈtägrəfē · macrophotography

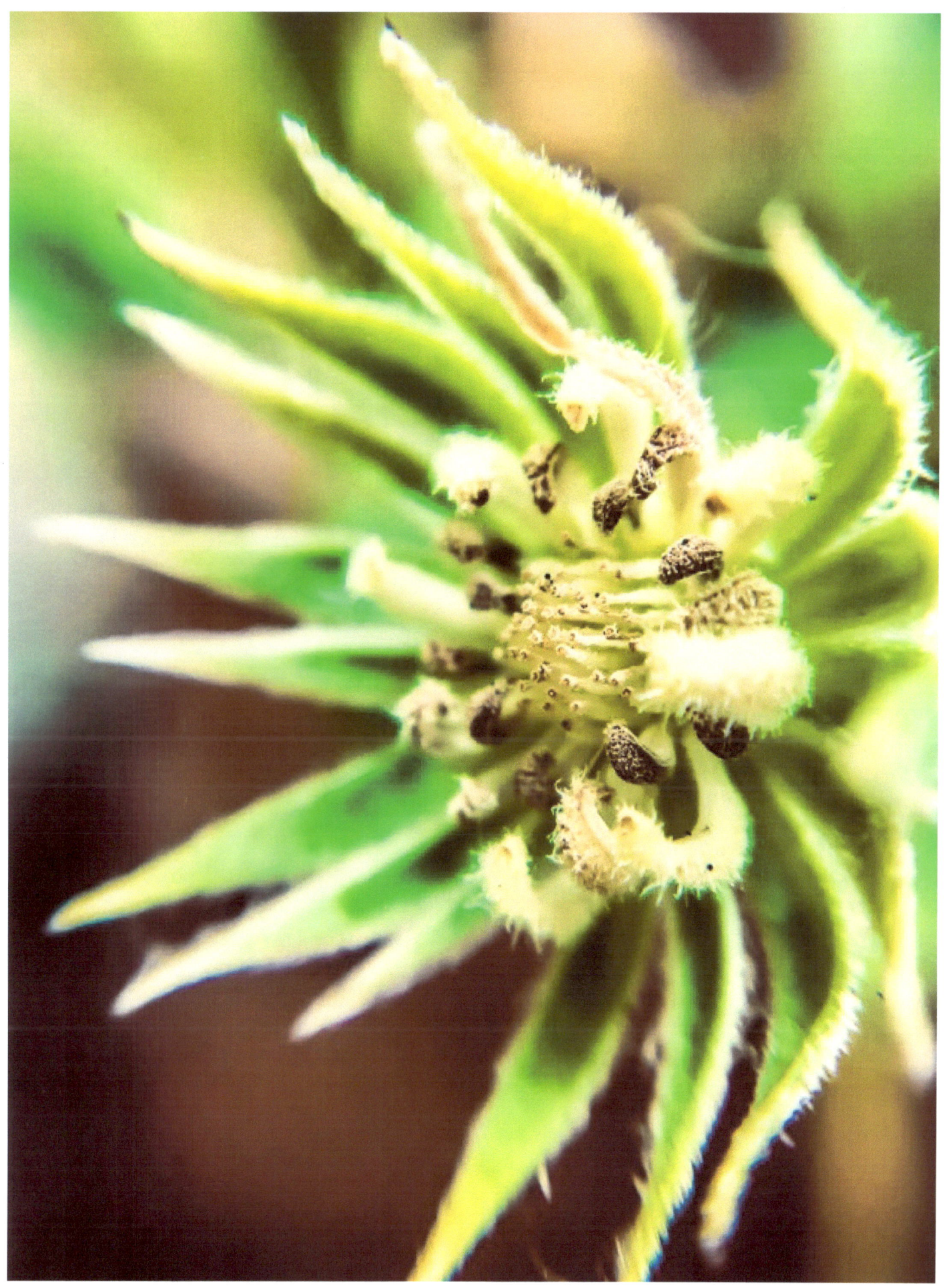

makrōfəˈtägrəfē  macrophotography

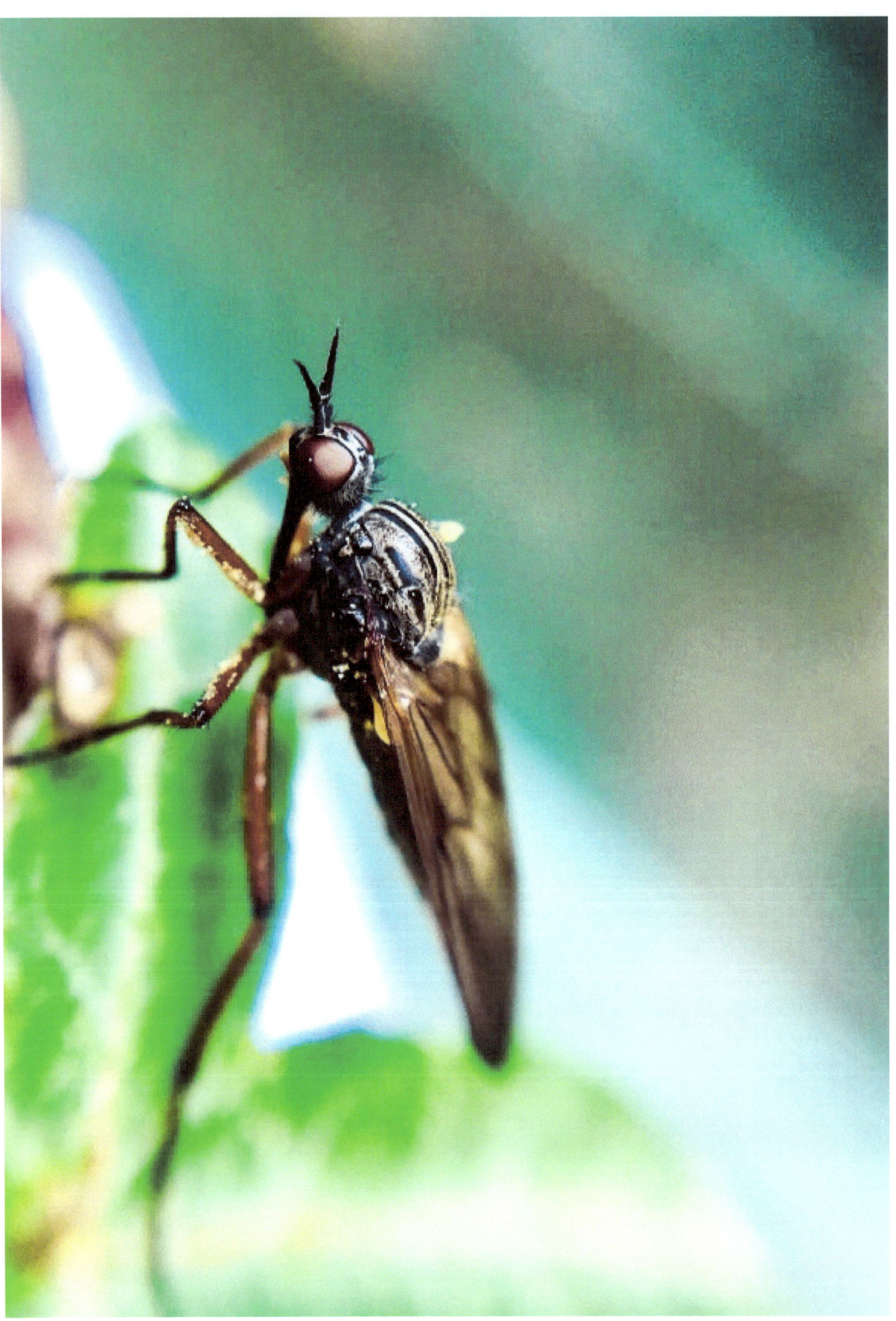

makrōfəˈtägrəfē macrophotography

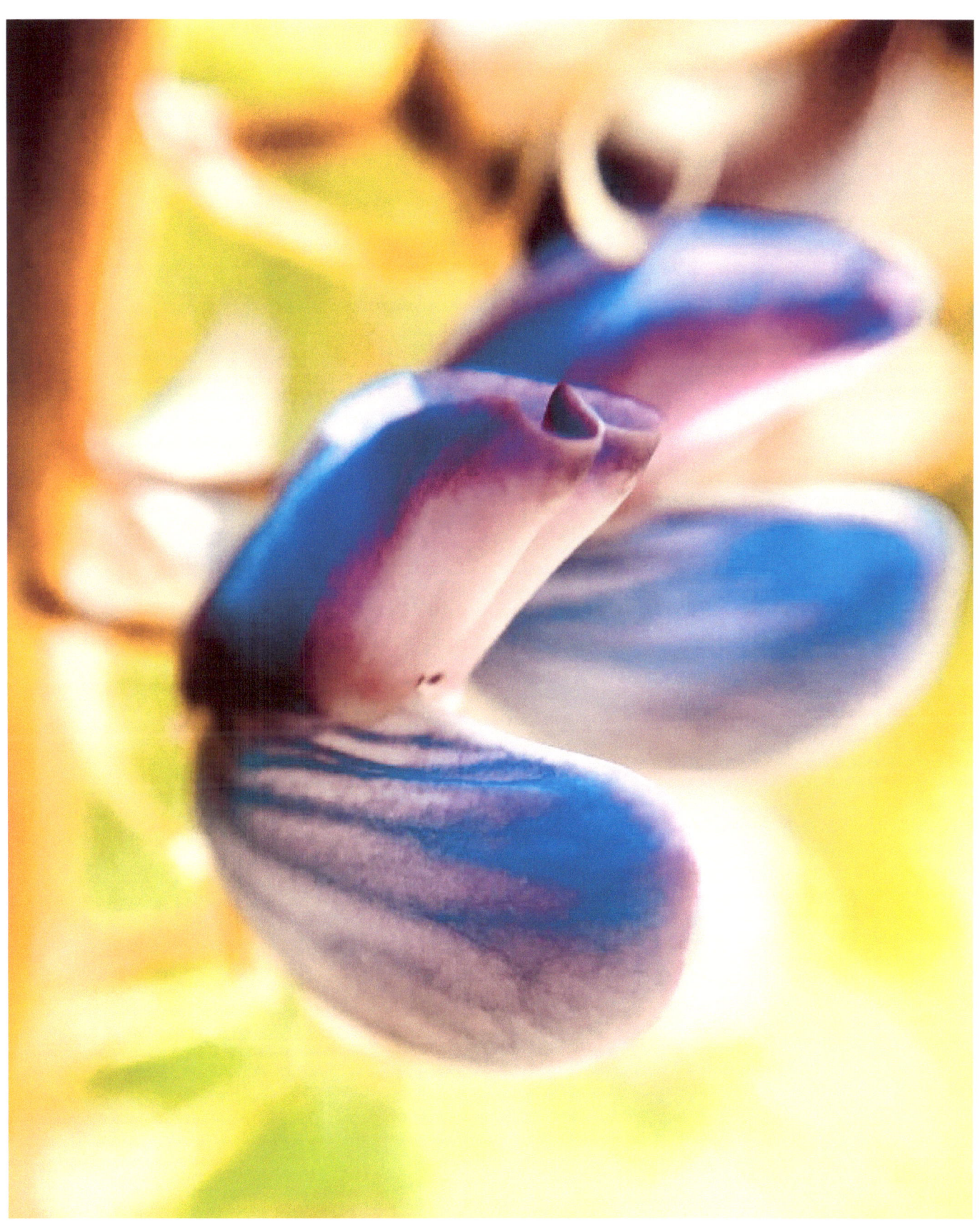

makrōfəˈtägrəfē · macrophotography

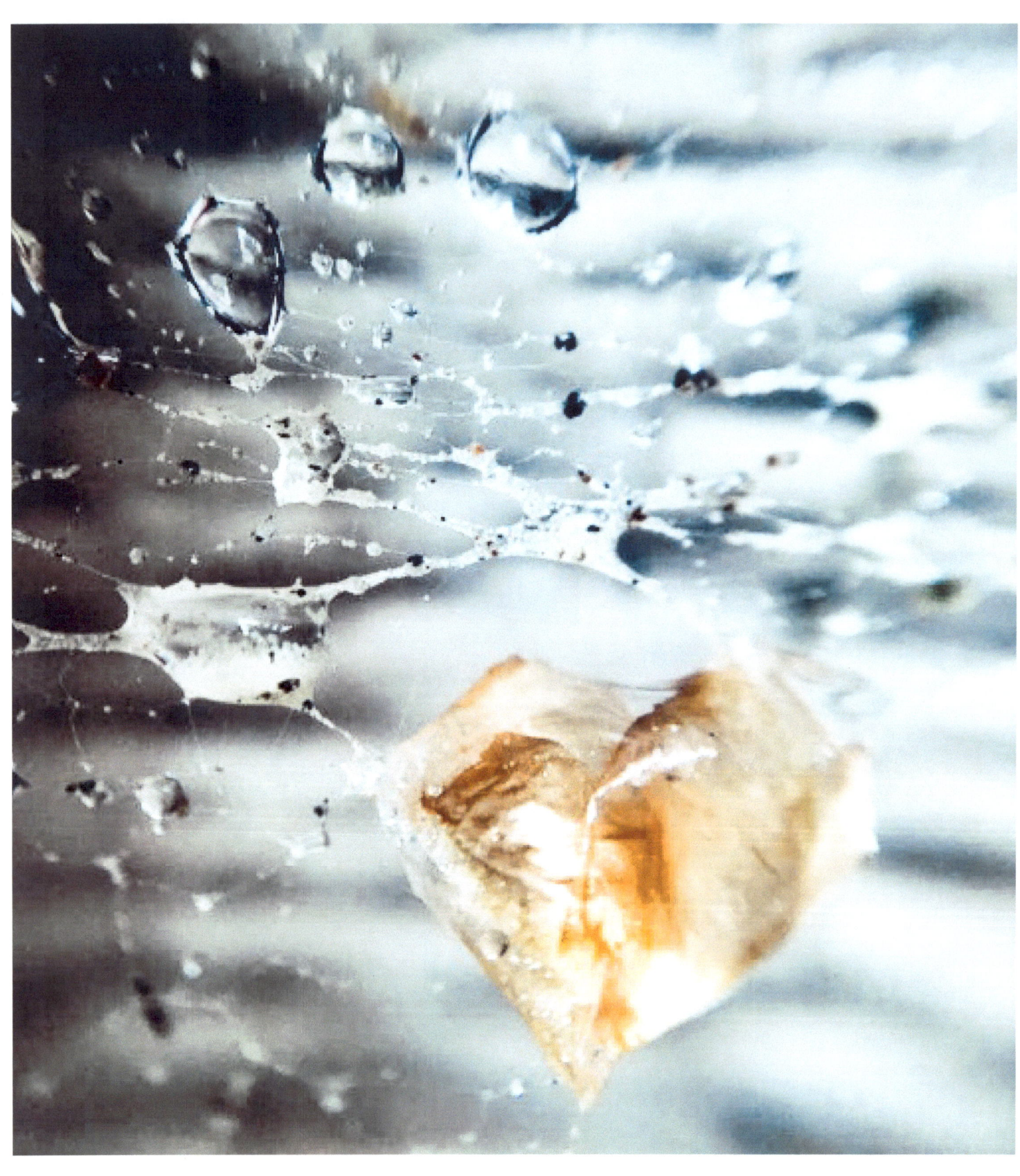

makrōfəˈtägrəfē            macrophotography

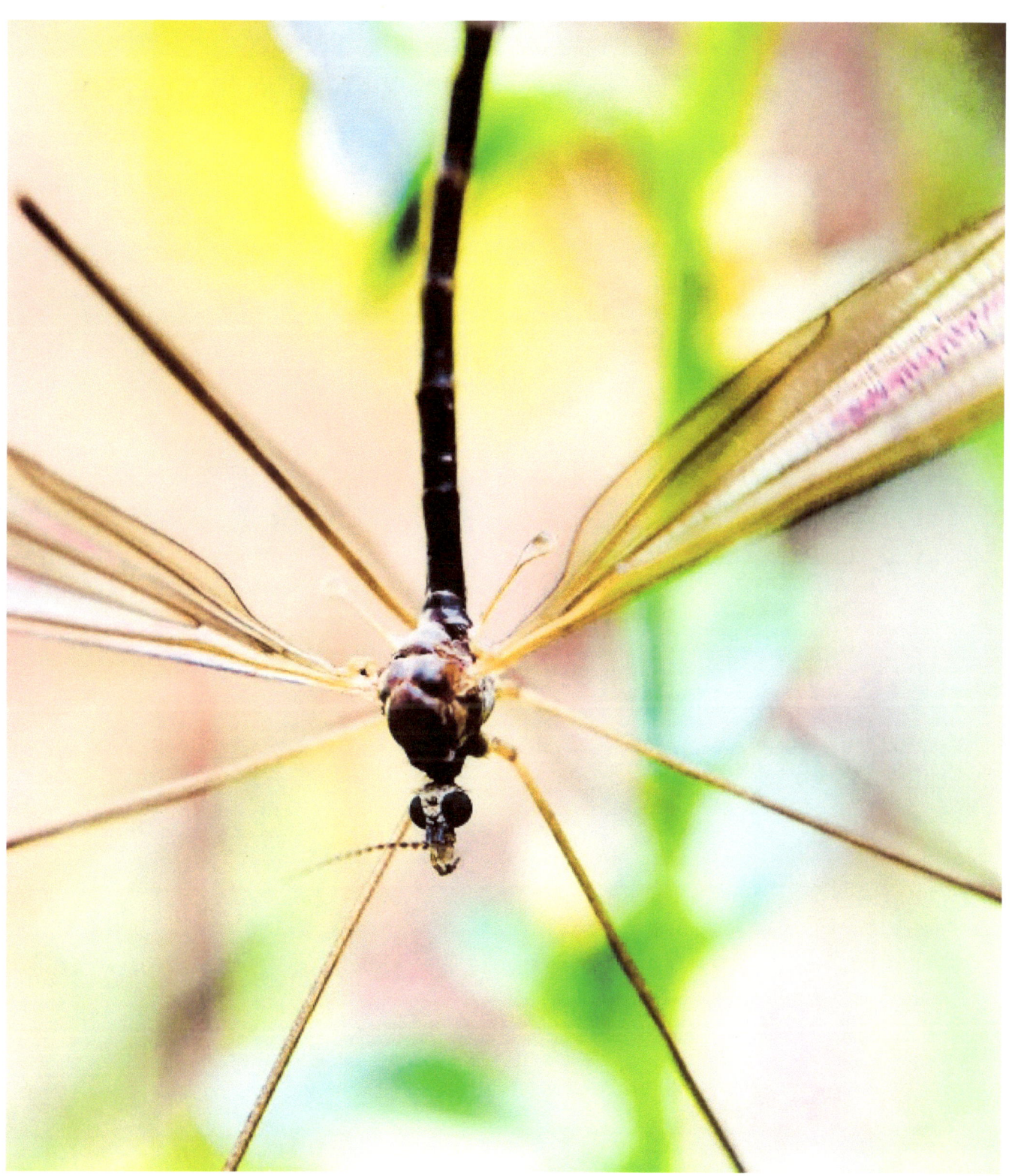

makrōfəˈtägrəfē macrophotography

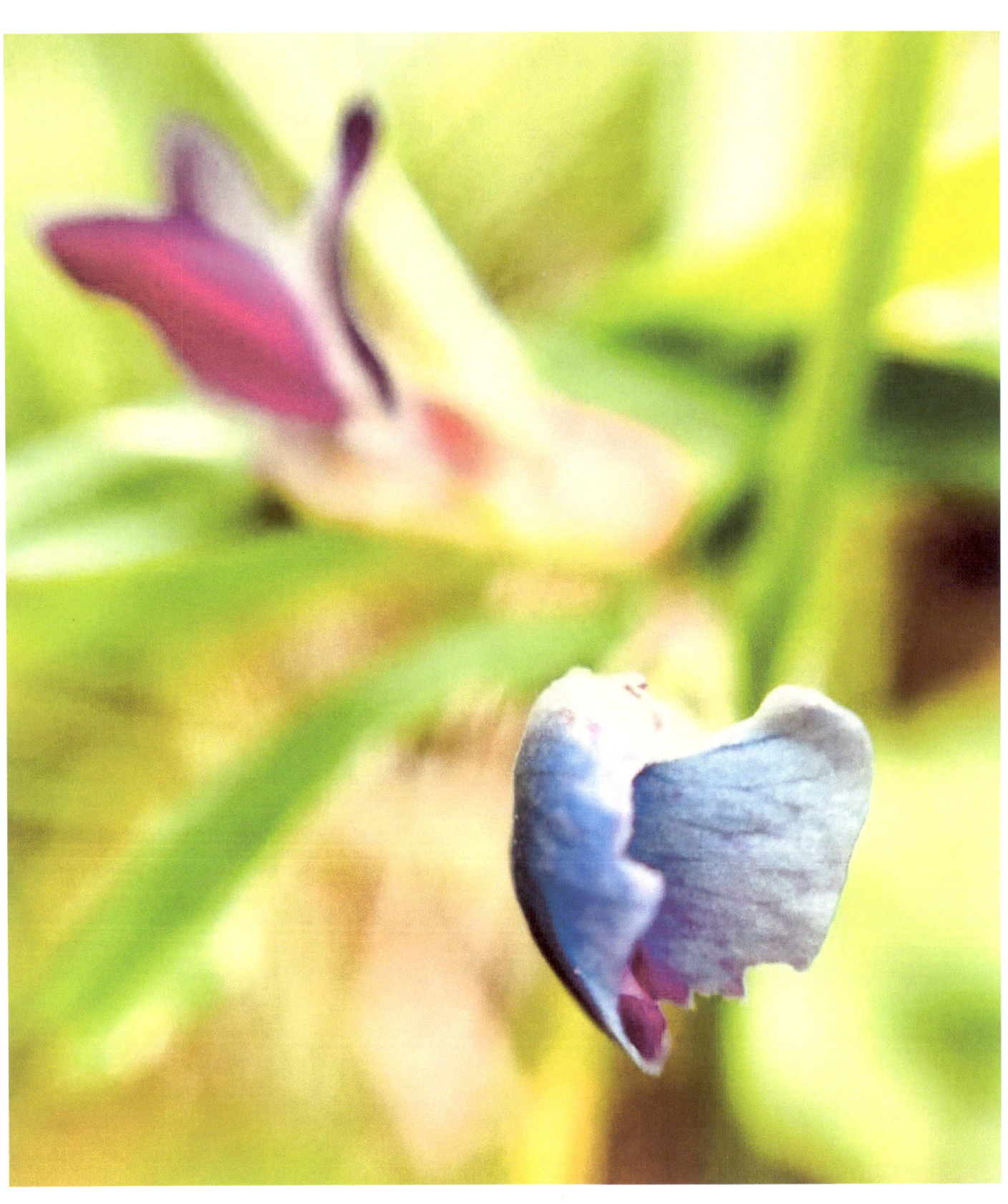

makrōfəˈtägrəfē · macrophotography

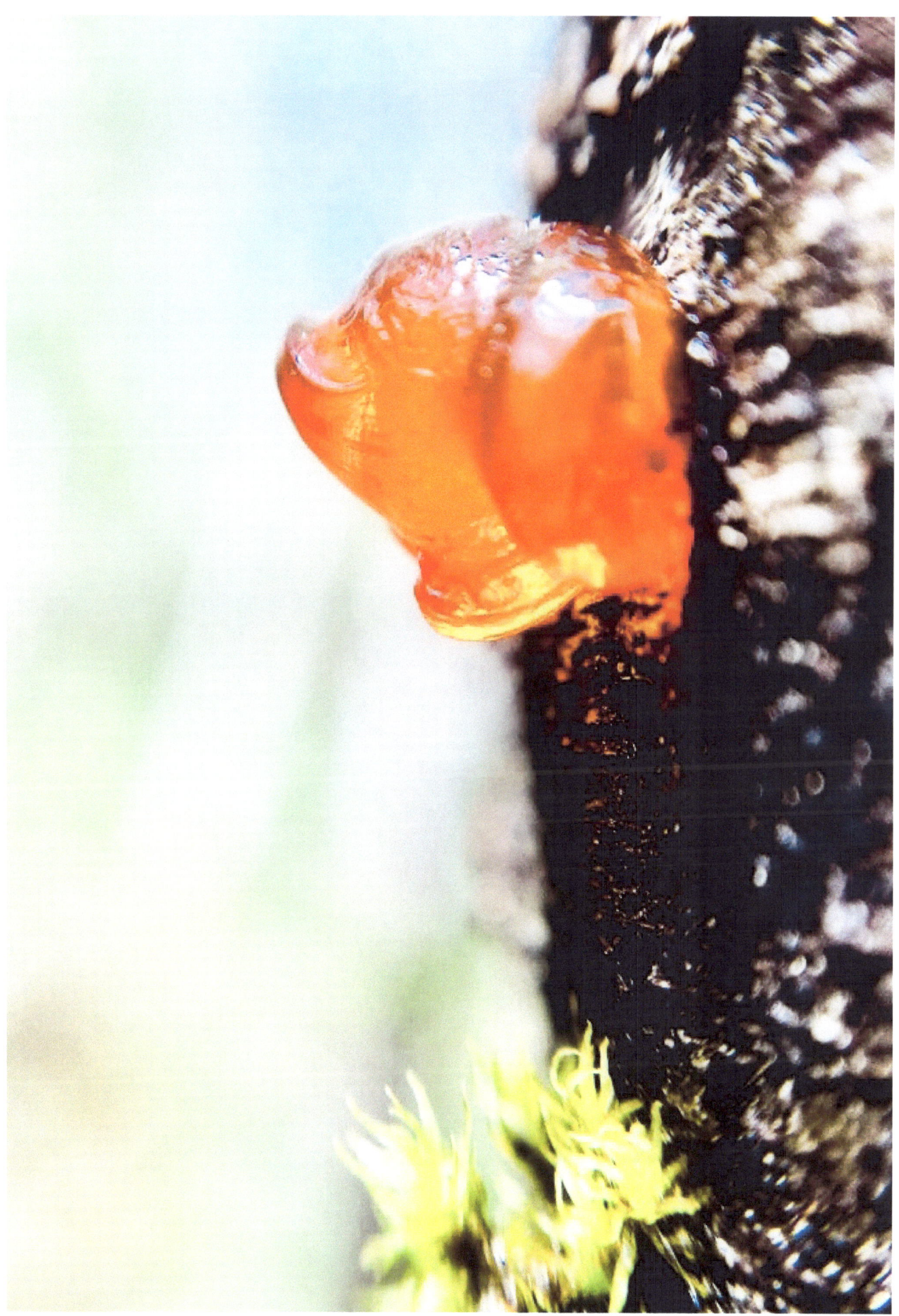

makrōfəˈtägrəfē        macrophotography

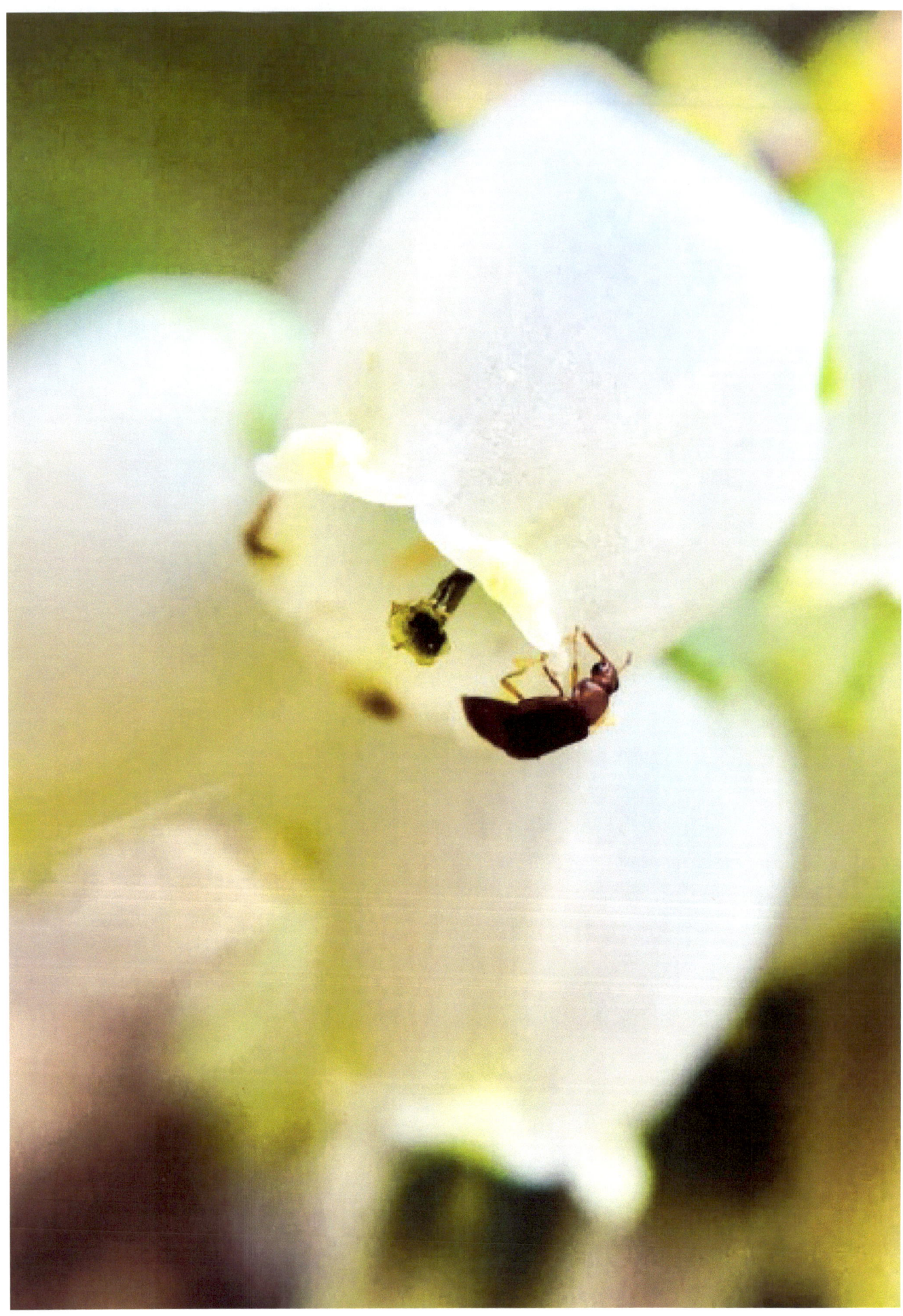

makrōfəˈtägrəfē · macrophotography

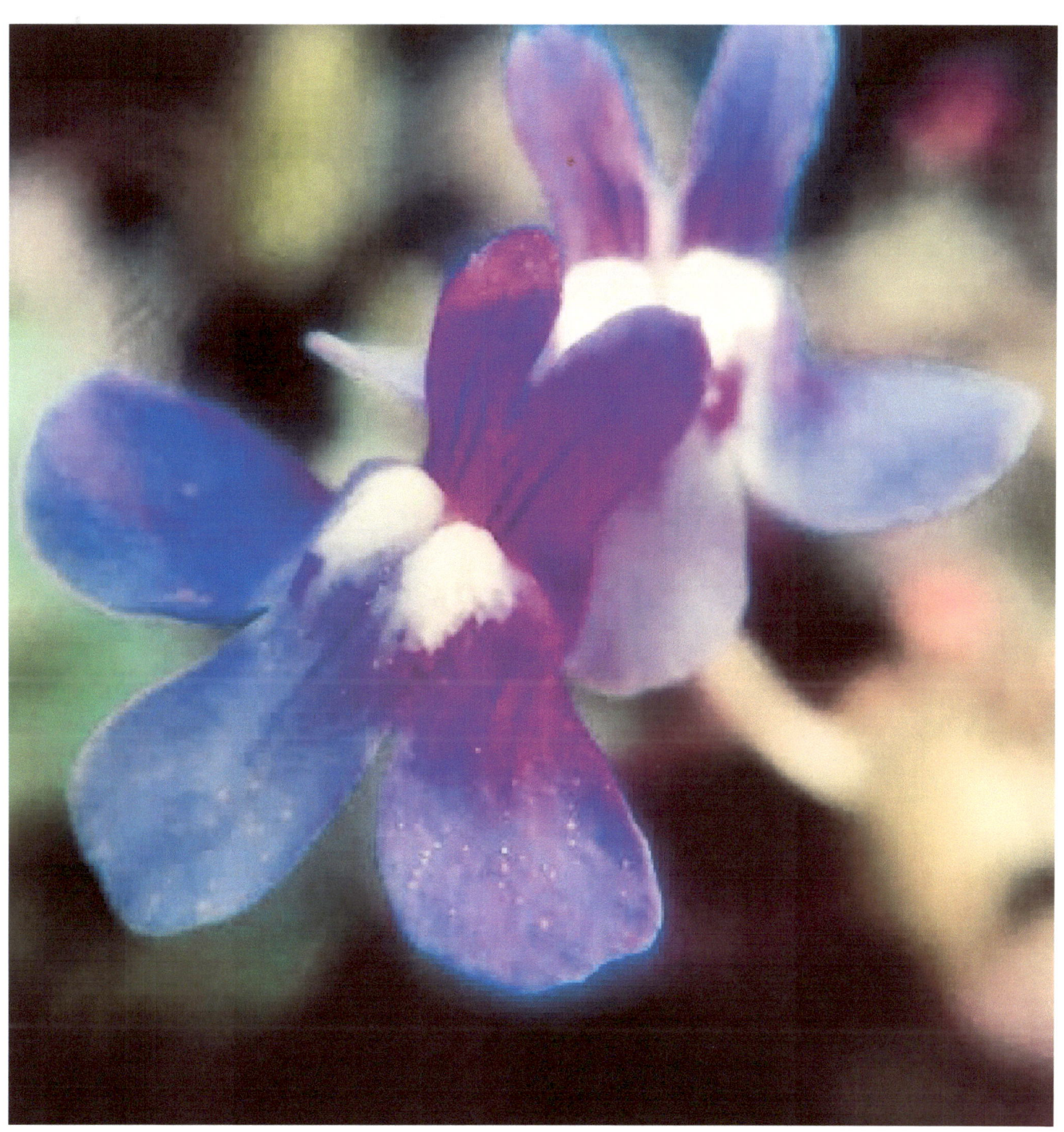

makrōfəˈtägrəfē  macrophotography

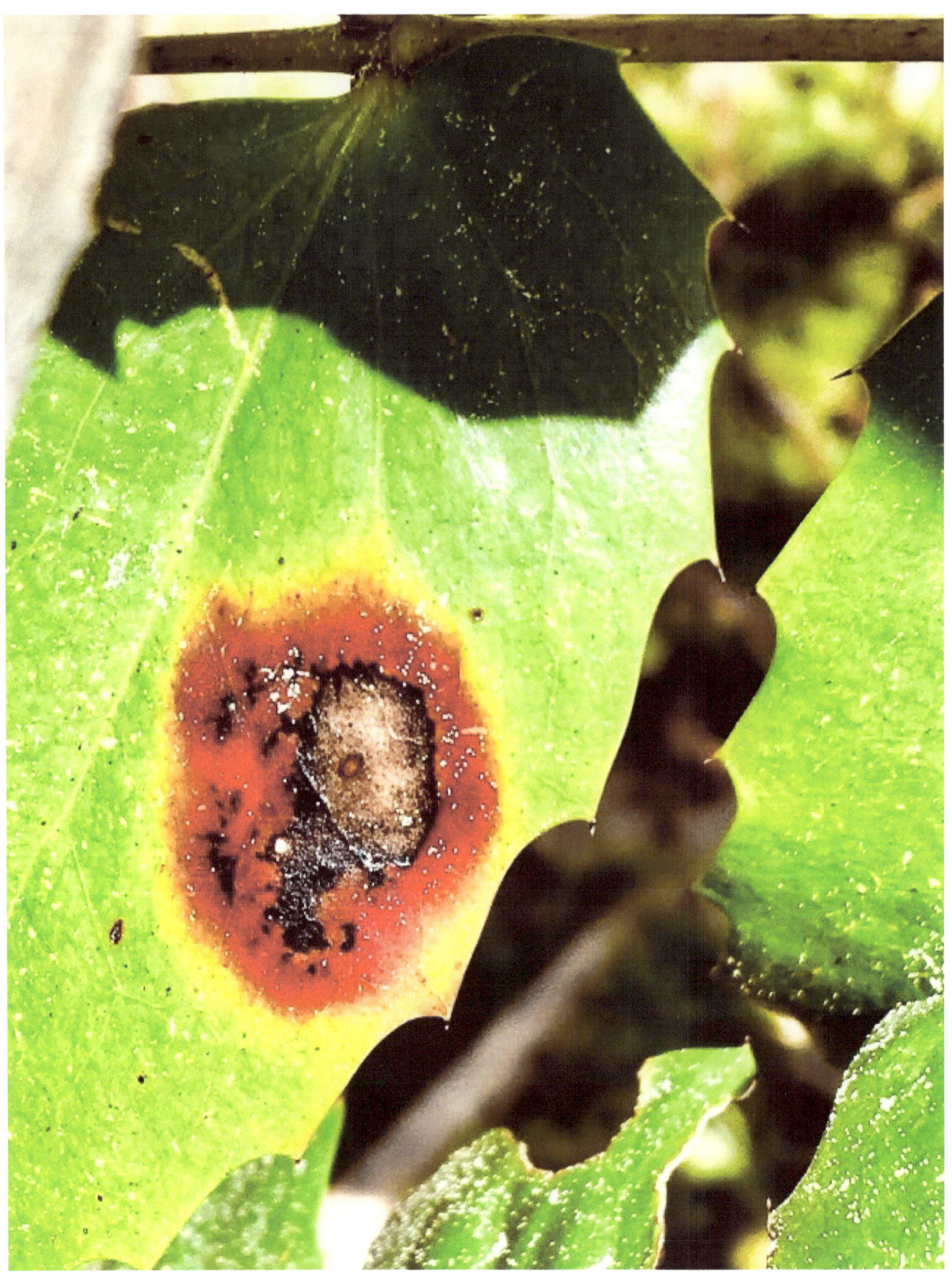

makrōfəˈtägrəfē    macrophotography

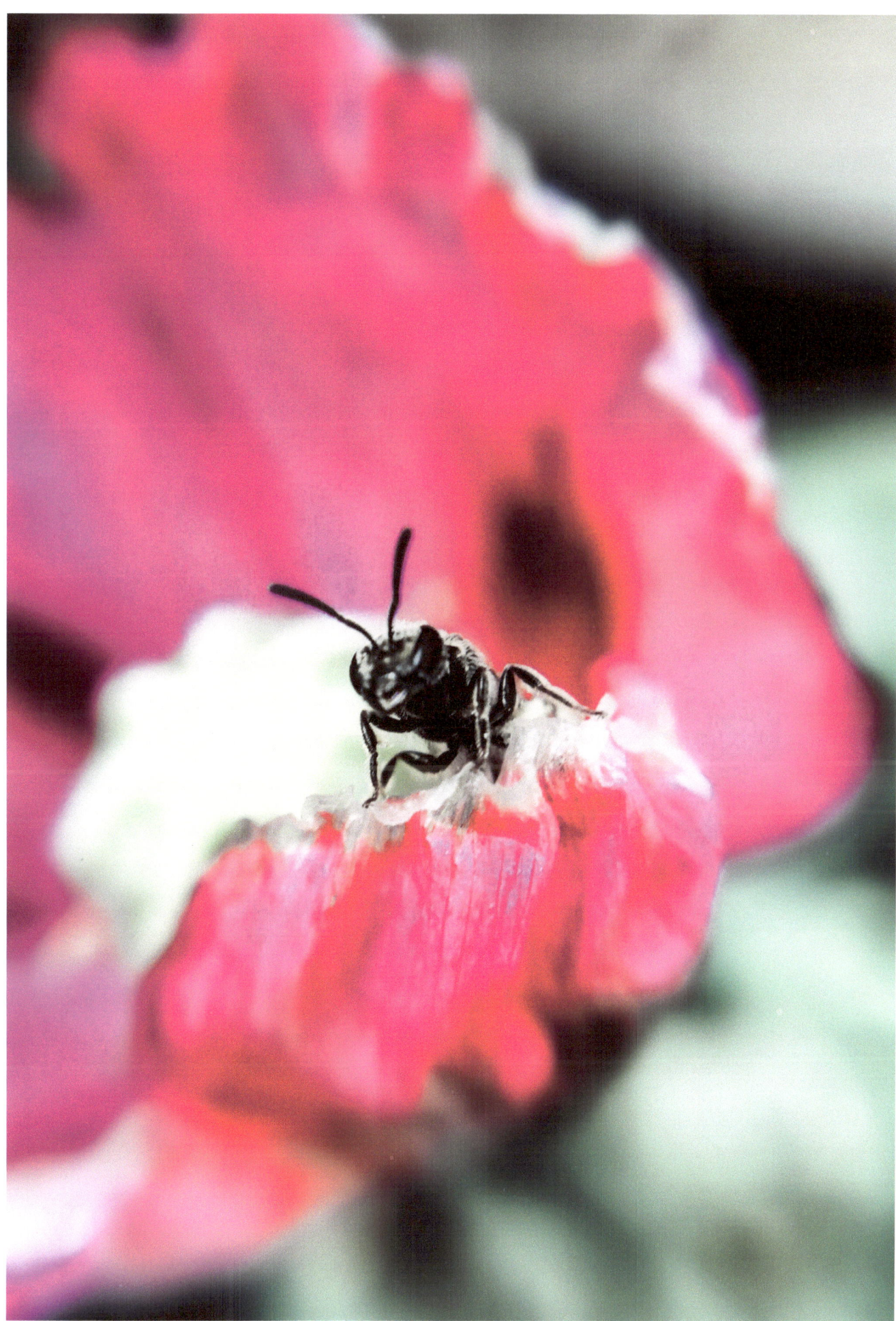

makrōfəˈtägrəfē · macrophotography

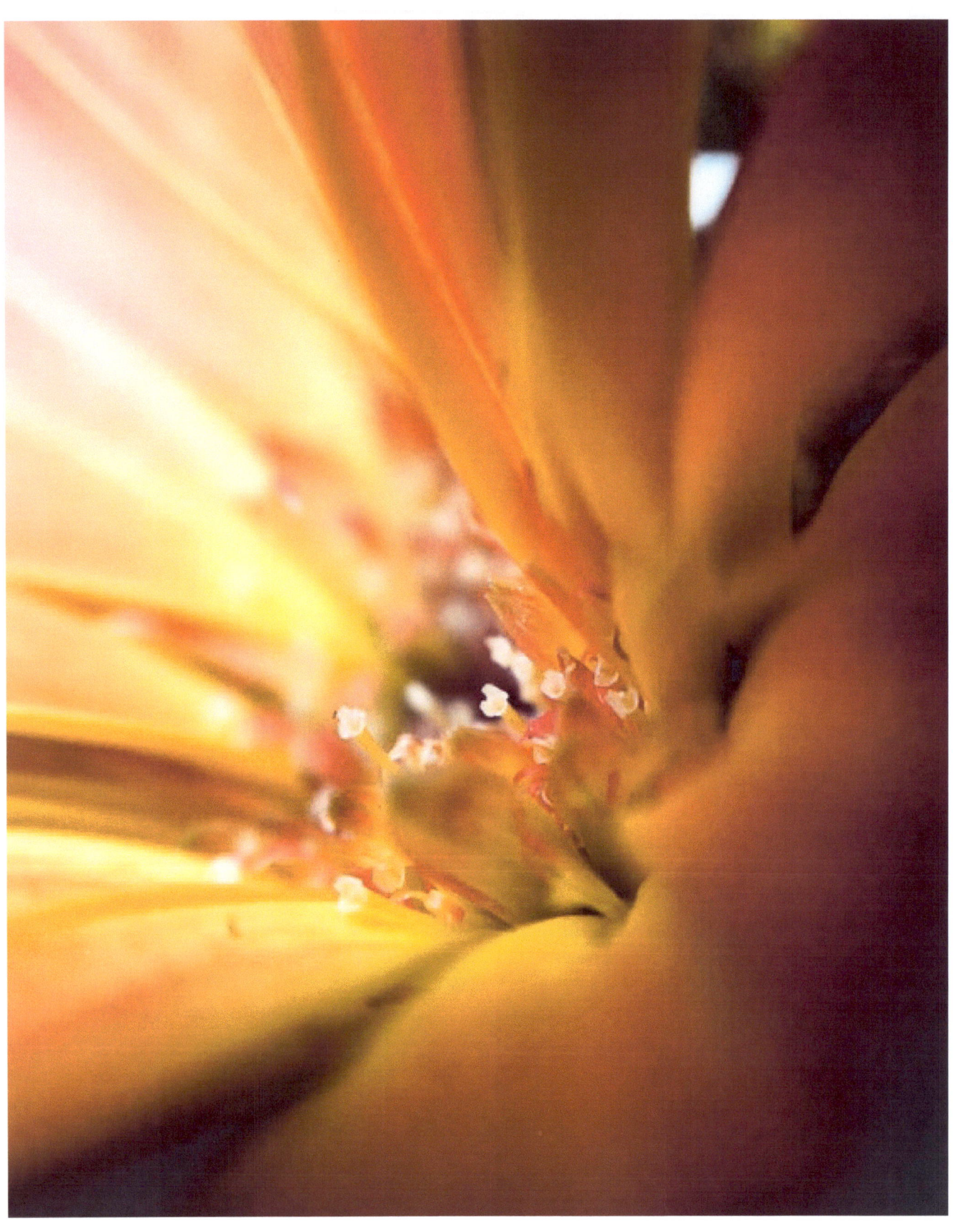

makrōfəˈtägrəfē · macrophotography

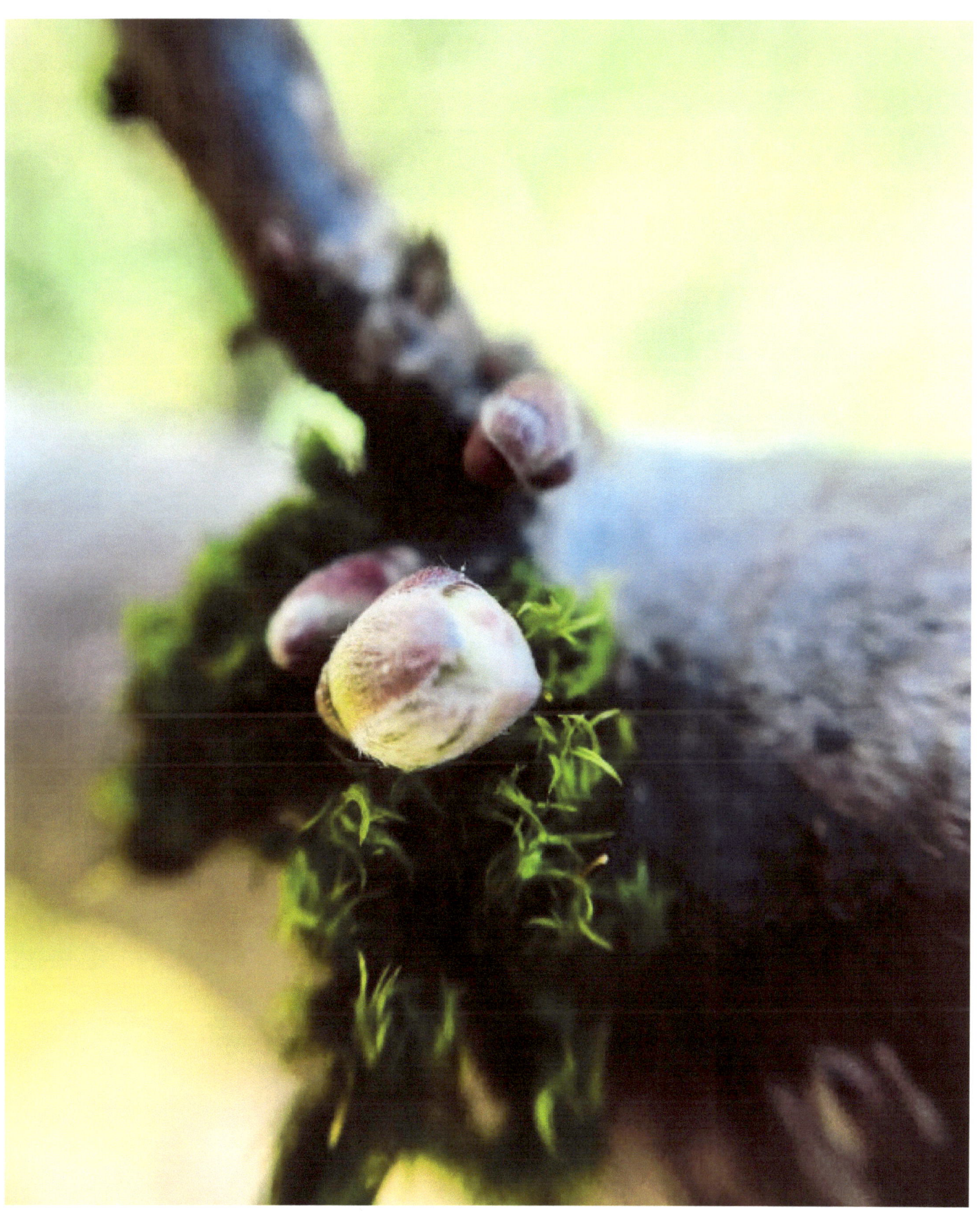

makrōfəˈtägrəfē　　　　　　　　　　　　　　　　　　　　　　　　macrophotography

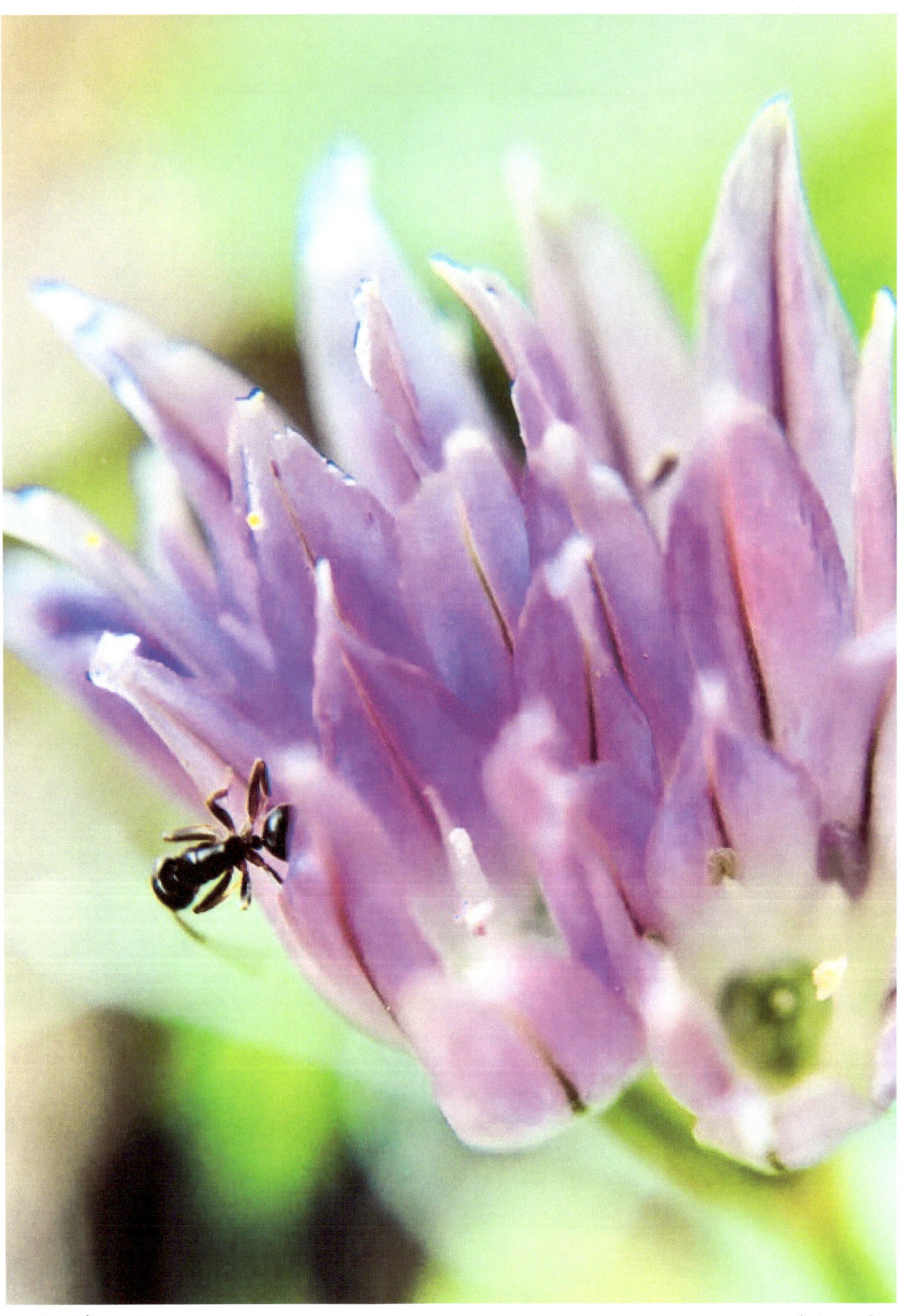

makrōfəˈtägrəfē　　　　　　　　　　　　　　　　　　macrophotography

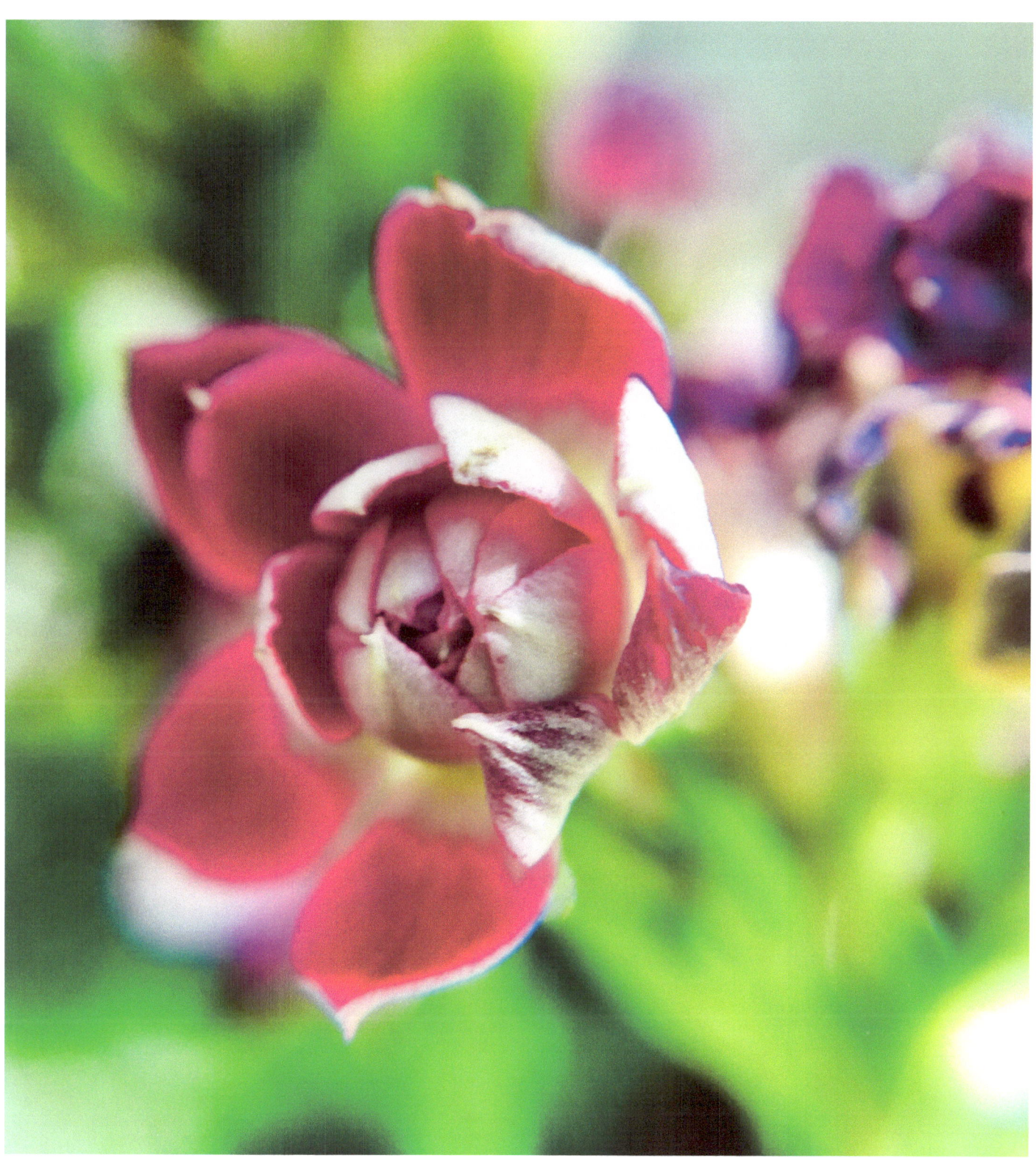

makrōfə'tägrəfē  macrophotography

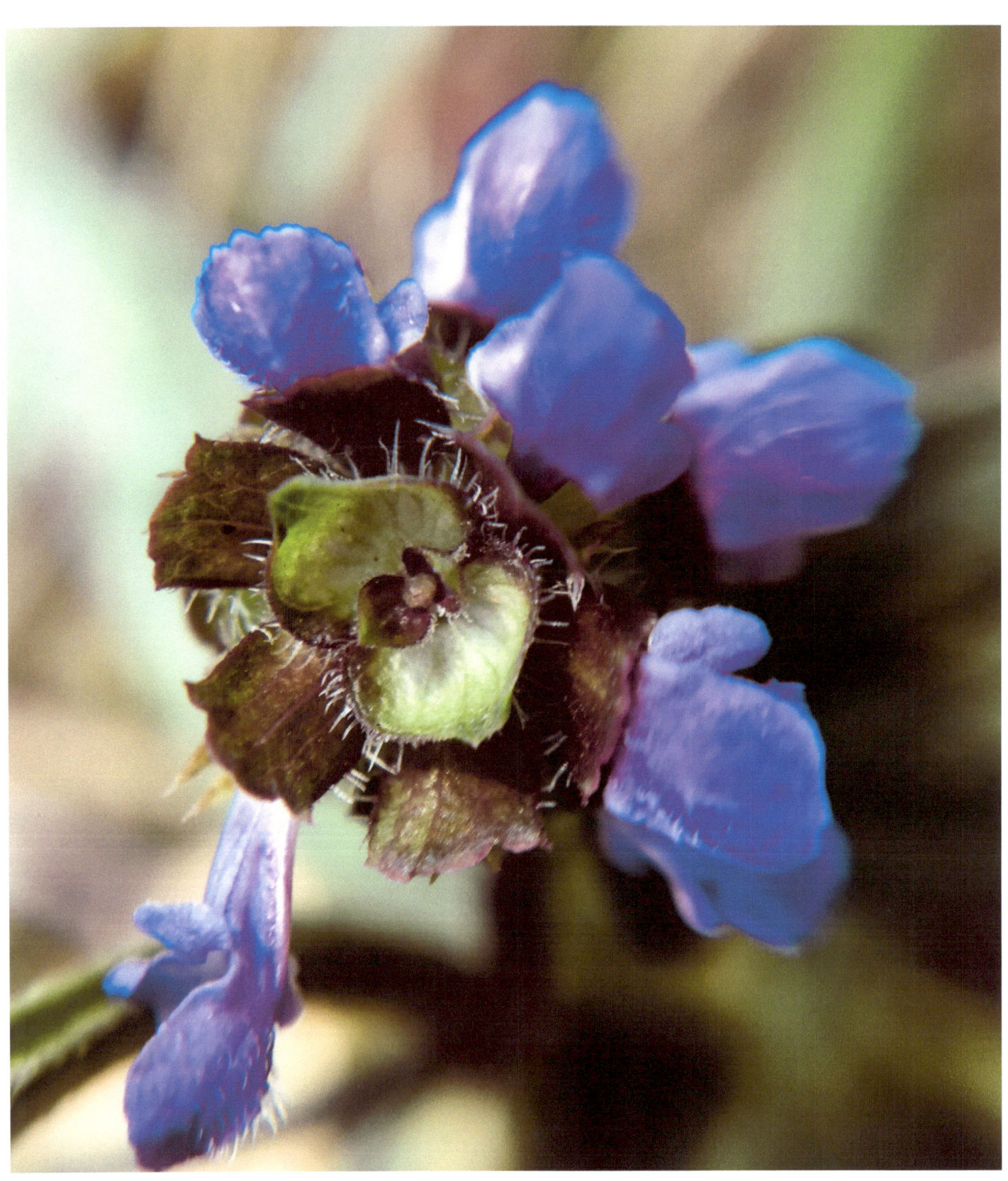

makrōfəˈtägrəfē · macrophotography

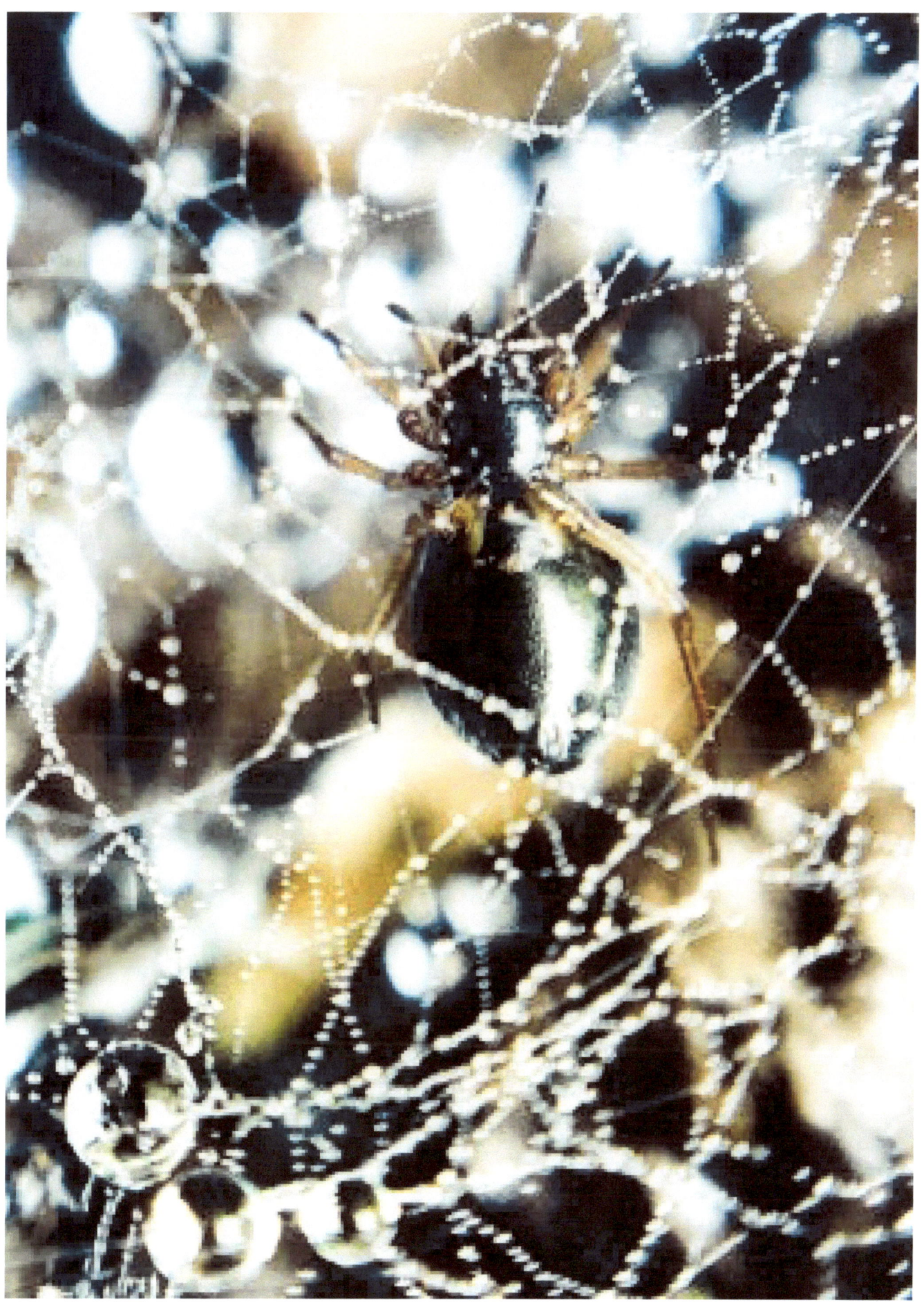

makrōfəˈtägrəfē · macrophotography

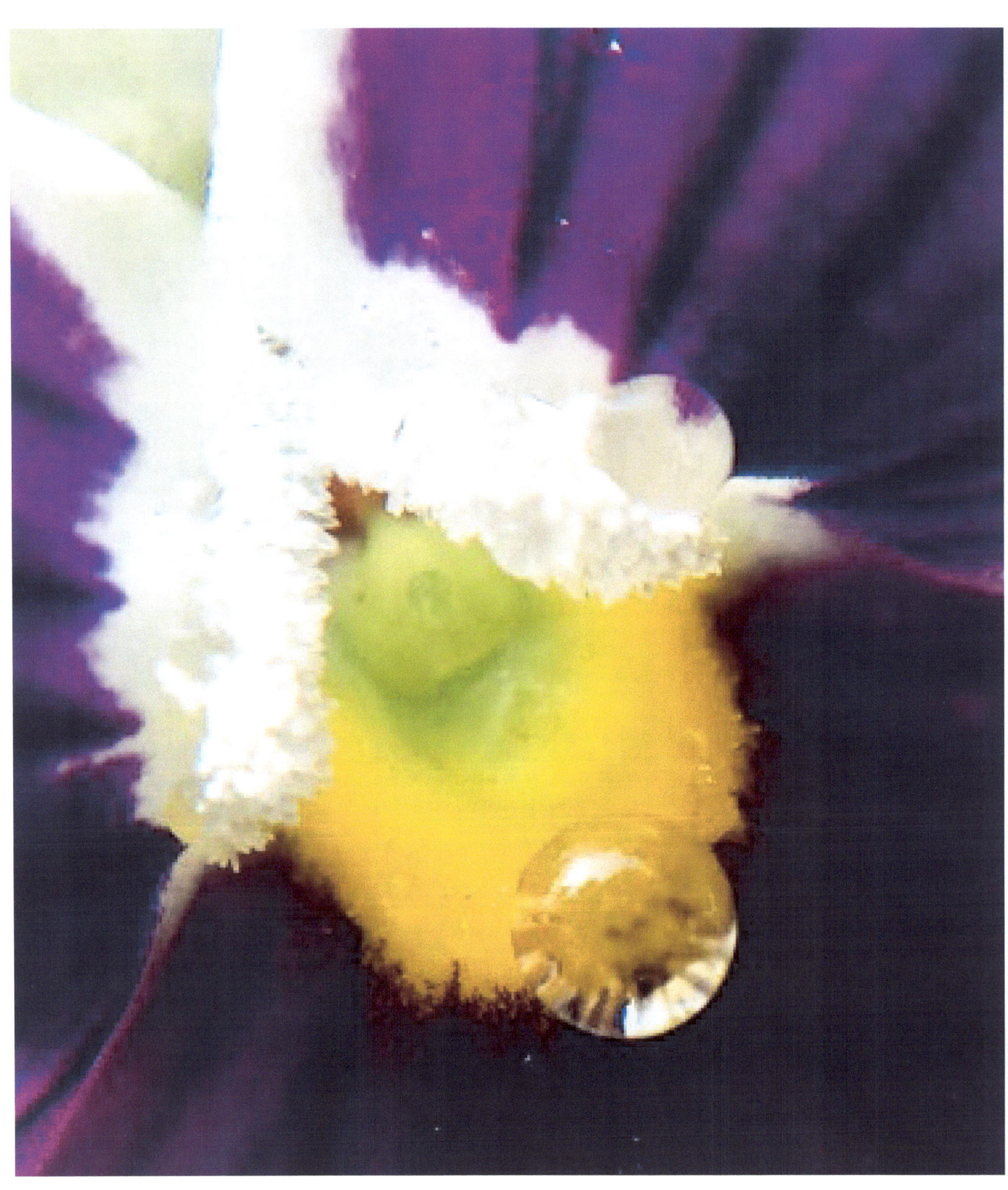

makrōfəˈtägrəfē        macrophotography

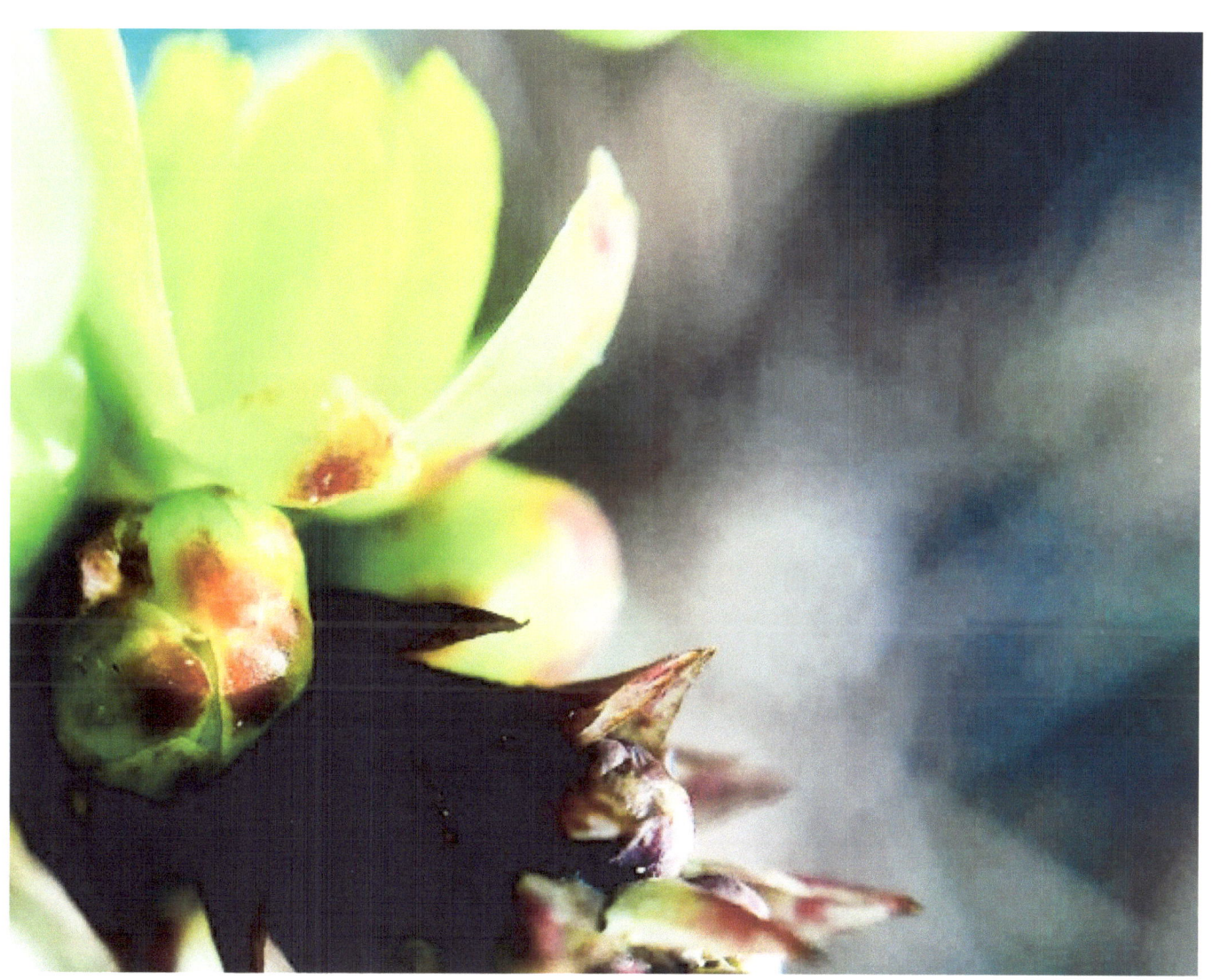

makrōfəˈtägrəfē · macrophotography

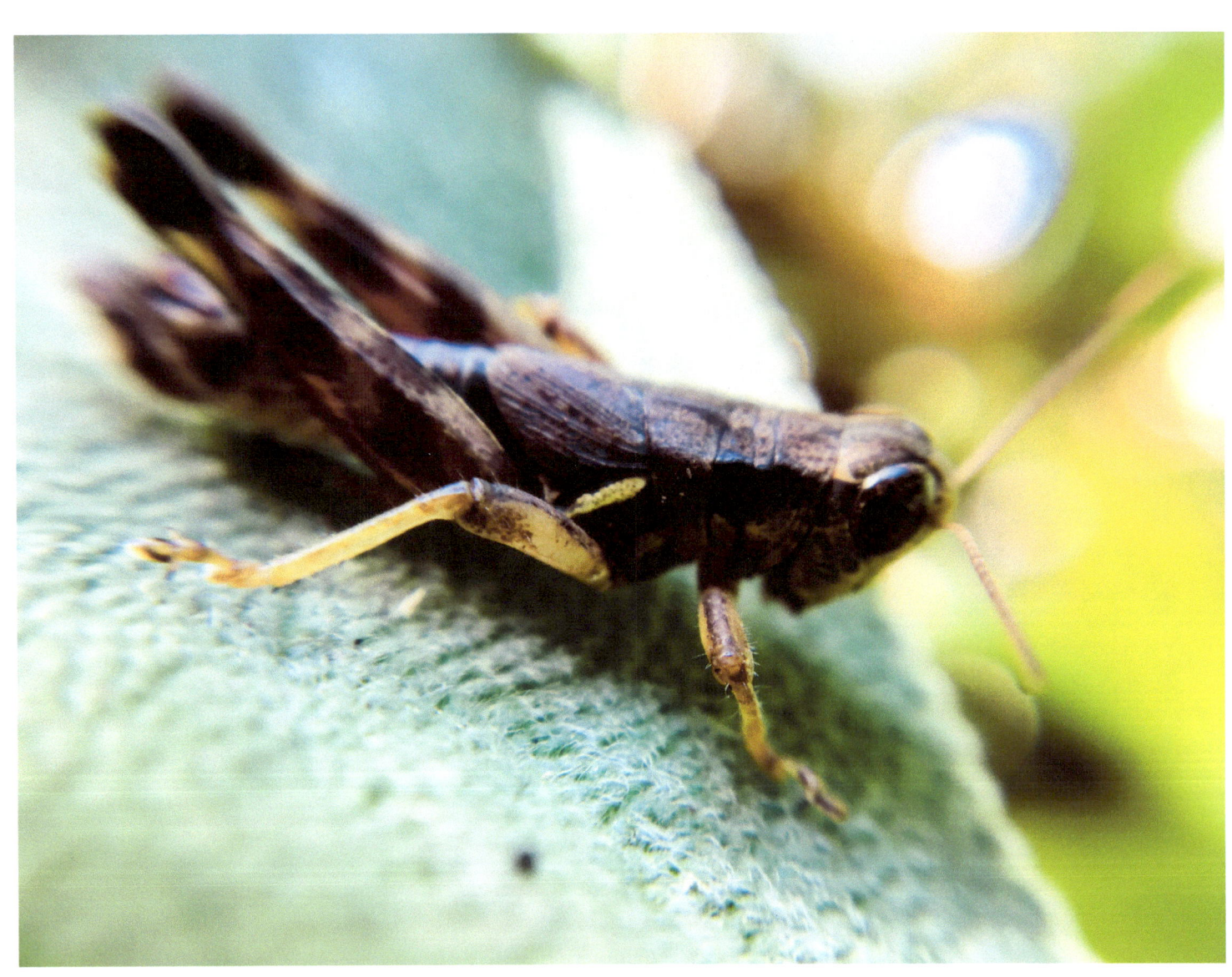

makrōfəˈtägrəfē  macrophotography

Meet the beauties immortalized in this photo album in order of appearance:

| | |
|---|---|
| Budding Talent | Al dente flora |
| Web Browser | Abstract on leaf canvas |
| Gold Rush | What's up? |
| East Face | The Last Dance |
| Black tie event | Webbed Droplets |
| Flying Oranje | Fly on Stilts |
| Thorny Beauty | Trionfo Violetto |
| Standing room only | Crown of Thorns |
| Ned the Arachnid | Straight ahead |
| Trifecta | LifeCycle |
| When I grow up | Propeller |
| Moth on Moss | Frequent Flyer |
| Morning Stretch | Ms. Pac-Man and Friend |
| Swirling Pine | The Suspense of it all |
| It takes a Village | Mid-air |
| Taraxacum | Breaking up |
| That's a wrap! | Sapped |
| The Pollinator | The Visitor |
| Blurple | Blossom Buddies |
| Holey Leaf! | Beauty mark |
| Succulent and Fly | The Watcher |
| Diminutive Drop | Underneath it all |
| Blue | Moss n' Buds |
| In the Limelight | Anybody home? |
| CoreBeauty | The Unfolding |
| PolkA_Dot | Prickly Purple |
| En route | Incognito |
| Unveiling | Dewey Pansy |
| Mellow Yellow | In Bloom |
| I see You | At ease |

makrōfə'tägrəfē                                               macrophotography

makrōfəˈtägrəfē  macrophotography